TWENTIETH CENTURY INTERPRETATIONS
OF
HARD TIMES

A Collection of Critical Essays

Edited by

PAUL EDWARD GRAY

Prentice-Hall, Inc. *Englewood Cliffs, N. J.*

A SPECTRUM BOOK

Contents

Introduction

by Paul Edward Gray

In June, 1854, Charles Dickens wrote to a friend: "But let us go somewhere, say to the public by the Thames where those performing dogs go at night. I think the travestie may be useful to me, and I may make something out of such an expedition; it will do us good after such a blue-devilous afternoon as this has been." [1] *Hard Times* was appearing in weekly segments in *Household Words*, a periodical Dickens himself edited, at the time this invitation was issued, and the "something" Dickens hoped to "make out of such an expedition" evidently involved the description of Sleary's Horse-Circus that was to provide the background for the final events in his novel. (Four months earlier, he had written the same friend: "Will you note down and send me any slang terms among the tumblers and circus people, that you can call to mind?" [2]) Yet if Dickens contemplated this outing as an opportunity for research, he also felt the need for recreation ("it will do us good"), for the type of "Fancy" that Sleary's ménage represents in *Hard Times,* for a playful, if transient, escape from the responsibilities of earning a living. Such responsibilities weighed, in many ways, as heavily upon Dickens as they did upon the Coketown laborers he portrayed in the pages of *Hard Times.*[3]

Dickens was born, in 1812, into a social and economic *milieu* in which "Fancy" was noticeably lacking. His father, an unsuccessful civil servant, was an erratic provider for his family, and Dickens's early years were spent travelling from one minor government out-

[1] Letter to Mark Lemon, quoted in *The Letters of Charles Dickens,* ed. Walter Dexter (Bloomsbury: The Nonesuch Press, 1938), II, 560.

[2] Letter to Mark Lemon, quoted in *Letters,* II, 542.

[3] The biographical details in this essay are based on Edgar Johnson, *Charles Dickens: His Tragedy and Triumph* (New York: Simon and Schuster, Inc., 1952), 2 vols. There is as yet no standard edition of *Hard Times*; references to the novel in this essay will be given, in parentheses, as Book and Chapter numbers.

1

post to another, gaining what education he could from a voracious reading of novels and tales. At age 12, the boy was forced to work for three months in a blacking factory, pasting labels on bottles, while his father languished in prison for debt; the specter of this humiliating experience and its attendant poverty haunted Dickens for the rest of his life. Hard work drove him through brief careers as a court stenographer and newspaper reporter and led him, eventually, to write novels, a task at which he worked harder than ever. In the eighteen years preceding the publication of *Hard Times,* Dickens had produced nine full-length novels under the relentless pressures of weekly or monthly deadlines. He had also published a collection of newspaper pieces, *Sketches by Boz* (1836), a travel book, *American Notes* (1842), four Christmas stories, including *A Christmas Carol* (1843) and *The Chimes* (1844), a book for children, *A Child's History of England* (1853), and literally hundreds of newspaper and magazine articles on diverse subjects. He had served as editor of four periodicals, two of which, *Master Humphrey's Clock* and *Household Words,* he founded himself. He was probably the most famous English author of his age, but fame, which rewarded him handsomely, also burdened him with the task of maintaining his popularity and the standard of living to which he, his wife, his nine children, and assorted relatives and in-laws had become accustomed. Dickens learned, as had Daniel Defoe and Tobias Smollett a century earlier, that an idle pen produced no income, a maxim with which Thomas Gradgrind of *Hard Times* would certainly agree; this discovery in part explains his willingness to assume editorial posts that assured him a relatively stable salary while promising some relief from the necessity of constant creative effort.

In the case of *Household Words,* this stratagem was not entirely successful. In August, 1853, Dickens wrote the last words of *Bleak House,* a long, intricate, and ambitious work that had been appearing monthly since March, 1852, and he decided to take a year's respite from the writing of fiction, the first substantial vacation from his novels that he had had since 1842. The publishers of *Household Words,* however, were becoming concerned about the declining sales of their journal at the same time that Dickens was contemplating a year of relative leisure, and they were convinced that a new Dickens novel in the issues of *Household Words* would cure that periodical's ailing circulation. ". . . There is such a fixed idea on the part of my partners and co-partners in Household Words," he wrote on January 23, 1854, "that a story by me, continued from week to week, would make some unheard of effect with it, that I am going to write one." [4] That same day he wrote the first words of *Hard Times*. "I did intend," he noted to a friend two months later, "to be as lazy as I could be through the summer, but here I am with my armour on again." [5] Given these circumstances, Dickens's desire for diversion, for "Fancy," during the spring and early summer months of 1854 is understandable; given, on the other hand, his amazing energy and his ultimate faith in the economic system that prodded him on to these new exertions, Dickens's prudent plan to "make something out of" his entertainment that June evening is understandable as well.

For the enemy that Dickens attacks in *Hard Times* is not, as a number of readers have assumed, Victorian society or its institutions as such. This novel ridicules, instead, the excessive or oppressive uses to which these institutions are put. Coketown is an ugly, dirty, monotonous, joyless place, not unlike Manchester, which Dickens thought of as the model for Coketown, or a number of other factory sites that sprang up in England between 1770 and 1840, sooty progeny of the Industrial Revolution; but *Hard Times* does not challenge the fundamental necessity of Coketown's existence, only its right to be ugly, dirty, monotonous, and joyless. Nowhere in *Hard Times* is there an intimation that the product of the Coketown mills could be dispensed with. Dickens simply argues that Coketown should be a better, a more attractive and humane place than it is. Josiah Bounderby may be a vicious enemy of the people, but he is not, in the world of this novel, an Enemy of the State to be haled before a revolutionary firing squad. The extent of Bounderby's punishment is a repudiation by shabby aristocracy, in the person of Mrs. Sparsit, the loss of his none-too-affectionate wife, and a contested will after his death. The justice meted out to Bounderby is poetic, not social. And Dickens revealed his private attitude toward the matter-of-fact, utilitarian Thomas Gradgrind in a letter of June 17, 1854, to Henry Cole, Secretary of the British Department of Science and Art:

I often say to Mr. Gradgrind that there is reason and good intention in much that he does—but that he overdoes it. Perhaps by dint of

[4] Letter to Angela Burdett-Coutts, quoted in *The Heart of Charles Dickens,* ed. Edgar Johnson (New York: Duell, Sloan and Pearce; Boston: Little, Brown and Company, 1952), p. 258.
[5] Letter to Emile de la Rue, quoted in *Letters,* II, 545.

his going his way and my going mine, we shall meet at last at some halfway house where there are flowers on the carpets, and a little standing-room for Queen Mab's chariot among the Steam Engines.[6]

Dickens and Gradgrind do meet in the final chapters of *Hard Times,* where the latter emerges as a genuinely sympathetic, if defeated, character. The author's agreement with Gradgrind's ends may be obscured by the satire of his utilitarian methods in the opening chapters, but that agreement is nonetheless manifested in the novel. Dickens's narrative vision of Louisa Gradgrind's future, of her "trying hard to know her humbler fellow-creatures, and to beautify their lives of machinery and reality . . ." (III, ix), is only an emotional amelioration of Gradgrind's view of life, a view in which "machinery and reality" factually, irrefutably have their place.

Not surprisingly, Dickens's middle-of-the-road position in *Hard Times* has drawn controversy from two sides. Conservative Victorian critics argued that Dickens wilfully exaggerated the evils of industrialism and "practical" education and that he misunderstood the principles of *laissez-faire* economy set forth by men such as Jeremy Bentham (1748–1832) and James Mill (1773–1836). Writing on the "fallacies" in *Hard Times,* a critic named Edwin P. Whipple took this approach in 1877: "Whatever Dickens understands he humorously represents; whatever he does not understand he humorously misrepresents. . . ."[7] Whipple portrayed Dickens as a sentimentalist railing against facts of life that practical men recognize as natural and beneficent:

. . . Dickens's mind was so deficient in the power of generalization, so inapt to recognize the operation of inexorable law, that whatever offended his instinctive benevolent sentiments he was inclined to assail as untrue. . . . The great field for the contest between the head and the heart is the domain of political economy. The demonstrated laws of this science are often particularly offensive to many good men and good women, who wish well for their fellow-creatures, and who are pained by the obstacles which economic maxims present to their diffusive benevolence. The time will come when it will be as intellectually discreditable for an educated person to engage in a crusade against the established laws of political economy as in a crusade against the established laws of the physical universe. . . .[8]

[6] Quoted in Johnson, *Charles Dickens: His Tragedy and Triumph,* II, 797.
[7] Edwin P. Whipple, "Hard Times," *The Atlantic Monthly,* XXXIV (March, 1877), 355.
[8] Whipple, 353.

"Crusaders" such as John Maynard Keynes and Albert Einstein have cast retrospective doubt on Whipple's power of prophecy, and his argument against Dickens and *Hard Times* is equally debatable.

The question of how well Dickens understood industrialism, educational theory, and political economy is not particularly germane to a critical evaluation of *Hard Times*. If Bounderby succeeds or fails as a character in the novel, he does so not because Dickens had mastered the finer points of the utilitarian pleasure-principle but because the author succeeded or failed in creating a fictional context in which such a figure seems plausible. As a novelist, Dickens was under no obligation to prove that a flesh-and-blood counterpart of Bounderby existed in England in the 1850's, although he did, as will be suggested later, compromise this freedom at certain points in *Hard Times*; Dickens's responsibility was, instead, to *create* Bounderby, to translate an imaginative reality into a fictional character. To argue that a man like Bounderby never lived is, in one way, to praise Dickens's ingenuity as the creator of an imagined world.

"Ay, ay, ay! But you musn't fancy," the school-inspector tells Sissy Jupe in *Hard Times,* and those utilitarians who discount Dickens as a reliable social reporter have a similar disregard for fiction that masquerades as Fact. Such readers are, however, more vulnerable to contradiction than they acknowledge, for evidence indicates that some of Dickens's caricatures in *Hard Times* are pastel versions of the more colorful reality. M'Choakumchild and the educational practices he represents are bitterly castigated in the chapter entitled "Murdering the Innocents" (I, ii). Surely Dickens is here requesting a willing suspension of disbelief?

> . . . The time is nearly gone by, when children of seven and eight years of age are to be compelled to waste their time and their faculties on such preposterous and unsuitable exercises as enacting dramatic scenes, reciting parliamentary speeches, and reading the latest senti-mental poetry. The change of system is more deserving of gratulation, as it is as decidedly favorable to the morals as it is to the mental culture of our youth. It is truly deplorable to think of the amount of bad morality and false religion that must have been disseminated among the youth of this country, through the medium of school-books which were mainly compiled from such writers as Shakespeare, Chesterfield, and Hume.[9]

---

[9] This passage is reprinted in *Hard Times,* ed. George Ford and Sylvère Monod (New York: W. W. Norton & Company, Inc., 1966), pp. 306–7.

The above passage comes not from *Hard Times* but from the revised "Preface" to the thirty-seventh reprinting of *A Series of Lessons in Prose and Verse*, by J. M. M'Culloch (1801–83), an influential Scottish schoolmaster and minister. M'Culloch's textbook, which was first published in 1831, was honestly designed to correct certain inadequacies in British elementary education. Changes wrought by the Industrial Revolution were scarcely reflected in English classrooms during the early years of the nineteenth century, and M'Culloch was no doubt justified in his belief that oratory was poor preparation for a child to bring to the factory. By the time his book had been reprinted thirty-seven times, however, M'Culloch's belief had ossified into a natural law that placed "useless" items like imaginative literature far down the list of human necessities. As was so often the case, Dickens had his eye squarely on the excesses to which men like M'Culloch and his followers had been led, and M'Choakumchild is his fictionalized version of these excesses. M'Choakumchild is not "true" in the sense that Edwin P. Whipple would have applied that term, but neither is he "false," neither does he belong, as a writer for the *Westminster Review* claimed in 1854, to a class "of whose existence . . . no one is aware." [10] Those with eyes to see can perceive analogies between the fictional methods of M'Choakumchild in *Hard Times* and the literal methods recommended by M'Culloch in *A Series of Lessons*. M'Choakumchild's merits as a fictional character do not depend on these analogies, but the traditional assertion of Dickens's social naiveté is considerably weakened by them.

If conservative critics argued that Dickens went too far in *Hard Times,* commentators in the twentieth century have usually insisted that he did not go far enough. The inhumanity of an employer like Bounderby and the misery of a laborer like Stephen Blackpool are portrayed vividly enough. What many modern readers search for in vain is an ideologically acceptable resolution of the "muddle" that Stephen ponders. As a spokesman for the workers, Stephen claims to know what will *not* solve the dilemma portrayed in the novel:

> . . . The strong hand will never do't. Vict'ry and triumph will never do't. Agreeing fur to mak one side unnat'rally awlus and for ever right, and toother side unnat'rally awlus and for ever wrong, will

[10] *Westminster Review*, LXII (October 1, 1854), 605.

never, never do't. Nor yet lettin' alone will never do't. Let thousands upon thousands alone, aw leading the like lives and aw faw'en into the like muddle, and they will be as one, and yo will be as anoother, wi' a black unpassable world betwixt yo, just as long or short a time as sitch-like misery can last. Not drawin' night to fok, wi' kindness and patience an cheery ways, that so draws nigh to one another in their monny troubles, and so cherishes one another in their distresses wi' what they need themseln—like, I humbly believe, as no people the genelman ha' seen in aw his travels can beat—will never do't till th' Sun turns t' ice. (II, v)

Bounderby, to whom this speech is directed, responds by firing Stephen, thereby indicating the amount of "kindness and patience an cheery ways" he is prepared to distribute among his workers. Critics familiar with Marxist and Socialist doctrines are not in the least surprised by Bounderby's act; Stephen's plea for an iota of humanity from his employer is, they feel, pitifully irrelevant to the issue the novel *ought* to confront, *i.e.*, the process whereby the workers or the state relieve Bounderby of his possessions and eliminate, through force or legislation, what Stephen calls the "black unpassable world" between capital and labor. A philanthropic, glad-handing Bounderby would no more satisfy Marxist or Socialist yearnings than does the Bounderby in the novel, and writers such as George Gissing and George Orwell [11] have been annoyed by Dickens's refusal to exploit the revolutionary implications of his story.

Such critics expect more than Dickens ever promises in *Hard Times,* for he clearly condemns revolution as a disaster that human intelligence and benevolence must prevent:

Utilitarian economists, skeletons of schoolmasters, Commissioners of Fact, genteel and used-up infidels, gabblers of many little dog's-eared creeds, the poor you will always have with you. Cultivate in them, while there is yet time, the utmost graces of the fancies and affections, to adorn their lives so much in need of ornament; or, in the day of your triumph, when romance is utterly driven out of their souls, and they and a bare existence stand face to face, Reality will take a wolfish turn, and make an end of you. (II, vi)

The "wolfish turn" of Reality is not set forth as a promise to be fulfilled but as a warning to be avoided. This passage rests on sound utilitarian principles, and it is difficult to see why modern

---

[11] See the "View Points" section of this volume.

critics have imagined so much—and Victorian critics found so little—with which they could agree in *Hard Times*. Yet even those who do not read this novel as a stillborn revolutionary tract feel obliged to apologize for the portrait of Slackbridge, the demagogic union leader who attempts to organize the Coketown workers. Both Edgar Johnson and David Lodge, in essays reprinted in this volume, argue that Dickens failed to justify Stephen's refusal to join the United Aggregate Tribunal and that the treatment accorded Slackbridge is unfair. Discussing the account of Slackbridge's appearance before the Coketown assembly (II, iv), Johnson writes:

> Such a description is a piece of sheer ignorance, not because union leaders cannot be windbags and humbugs as other politicians can, but because labor organizers are not like Slackbridge and do not talk like him, and did not do so in Dickens's day any more than in ours.

Although the political perspectives differ considerably, this assertion is identical with that made in the *Westminister Review* concerning M'Choakumchild's nonexistence. Modern critics are, as a rule, sanguine about the caricatures of reactionaries such as Gradgrind and Bounderby, but they are made uneasy when the progressive force represented by Slackbridge is caricatured as well.

Yet the answer to Johnson's charge is the same as that given earlier to Edwin P. Whipple and the anonymous writer for the *Westminster Review*. Slackbridge is neither "true" nor "false" in a literal, denotative sense; he is a fictional character, an imaginative postulation of excesses that Dickens, at least, perceived as possible within the realm of human conduct. And Dickens had more contemporary evidence for his portrait of Slackbridge than Johnson's assertion suggests. Certain workers *were* complaining in the 1840's and 50's that the tyranny of their union leaders was as repressive as that of their employers; it was not unheard-of for a man to be ostracized from his fellow-employees by union edict, just as Stephen is sent into coventry by Slackbridge.[12] To the complaint that Dickens's picture of the labor movement is one-sided, one can only reply that his pictures of industrialism, education, and utilitarian economics are one-sided also. The modern

[12] For a brief account of such complaints, see R. K. Webb, *The British Working Class Reader: 1790–1840* (London: George Allen & Unwin Ltd., 1955), pp. 153–55. A disgruntled letter from one ostracized worker was printed in *The Times* of London on October 10, 1853; it is conveniently reprinted in the Ford-Monod edition of *Hard Times*, pp. 282–83.

view, that little *can* be said in favor of factories, "useful" education, and *laissez-faire* economics but that much *ought* to be said in favor of the trade unions, is as biased as the nineteenth-century view of Dickens the thoughtless rabble-rouser. Both judgments are founded on extraliterary, ideological considerations.

Hard Times has, since the moment it appeared, attracted an unusually heavy and sustained barrage of polemical fire. Nothing more clearly indicates the problematical relationship between the world of this novel and the world of an individual reader than the claims, made seventy-five years apart, that Dickens understood neither utilitarian economics nor labor organizers. Novels do not ordinarily provoke this kind of disagreement over literal truth, and it is interesting that *Hard Times* has been the catalyst of so much controversy. Historical and cultural changes between Dickens's age and the present do not adequately explain this phenomenon, for other of Dickens's novels, subject to the same changes, have been and are criticized in the type of political and social vacuum that *Hard Times* seems almost inevitably to fill. Dickens's narrative strategy in this novel evidently stimulates a reader's personal opinions and convictions in a manner that is worthy of some investigation.

Critics and experienced readers of fiction are customarily wary of identifying any fictional world too closely with the world it may pretend to reflect. A "naive" reader is one who expects fictional laws or ethical systems to coincide with his own; such a reader is likely to resent a sharp divergence between the fictional and his idea of the real. The "truth" of a novel, however, is not subject to the same laws of logic and evidence that govern discursive statements about the external or "real" world. The value of a newspaper story resides primarily in the event or circumstances that prompted its creation and that it claims to emulate; it is utterly dependent on elements outside of itself. The discovery that a murder did *not* occur profoundly affects the newspaper report of that murder. The discovery that the plot of a novel did not occur, on the other hand, is calmly accepted by all but the most utilitarian of readers. A novel is, in denotative terms, "false" at its outset. Consequently, novels do not *directly* appeal to or challenge a reader's beliefs about the world in which he lives. The newspaper story requires its readers to believe that a murder has taken place in their world; a novel asks its readers to believe that an event has taken place in its world. Novels can, and frequently do, change personal convictions, but they do so *indirectly*. Fiction asks only that its values be accepted as possible. Because it exists outside the realm of logical or scientific argument, a novel permits the reader to retain his personal beliefs while he considers fictional beliefs that may be contradictory to his own. The experience of holding, simultaneously, conflicting views of life can lead to a permanent accommodation of these views that alters the intellectual or emotional life of the reader.

The border between fiction and non-fiction, however, is extraordinarily difficult to define, and it is on this border that *Hard Times* takes its stand. For in this novel, Dickens asserts an unusually specific correspondence between his fictional world and the world of argument and debate in which he lived. He was not, apparently, satisfied with creating a world that was simply analogous to that of his own society. His impatience with abuses that he perceived around him compelled him to mingle external appeals with the internal laws of his fictional world, to waive, in essence, the novelist's freedom from the strictures of logic and evidence. As a result, *Hard Times* ranges unpredictably between self-enclosed art and denotative argument. It is neither completely self-dependent nor literally "true," and it is therefore peculiarly vulnerable to criticism on both aesthetic and historical grounds.

The clearest examples of Dickens's impatience with indirect, fictional persuasion are the numerous direct appeals his narrator makes to the reader, appeals based not on the imagined events within the novel but on external opinions or controversies:

> I entertain a weak idea that the English people are as hard-worked as any people upon whom the sun shines. I acknowledge to this ridiculous idiosyncrasy, as a reason why I would give them a little more play.
> In the hardest working part of Coketown; . . . (I, x)

This passage constitutes a temporary rupture in the self-enclosed world of the novel. The "English people" referred to in the first paragraph and the "Coketown" mentioned in the second belong to different orders of existence, but Dickens's narrator seeks here to abolish that difference. In so doing, he relinquishes the novelist's protection from literal contradictions, he burdens his fictional assertion with an external dependency. The passage opens Pandora's box on a question—Is Dickens correct? Are English people *actually* as hard-worked as any people in the world?—that could possibly, if pointlessly, be answered "no." Such an answer, accompanied by charts and tables, would resemble the factual wedges with which certain literalists have attempted to topple the entire novel. These efforts may be foolish and ill-conceived, but Dickens's own narrative strategy makes them possible and minimally respectable.

During Stephen Blackpool's first conversation with the mysterious Mrs. Pegler, he is asked whether the "troubles" she suspects he has follow him to Bounderby's factory:

> No, no; they didn't follow him there, said Stephen. All correct there. Everything accordant there. (He did not go so far as to say, for her pleasure, that there was a sort of Divine Right there; but, I have heard claims almost as magnificent of late years.) (I, xii)

This exchange conveys a puzzling mixture of attitudes. The narrator's repetitious assurances that the factory is ordered seem an ironic commentary on the mechanical, inhuman regularity of Bounderby's domain. Yet Stephen has already revealed, in the preceding chapter, his desperate desire to escape from these "troubles," the drunken wife with whom he is saddled. From Stephen's perspective, any relief from this situation, even if it be in the factory, should be considered a blessing. The narrator's attention, clearly, has been deflected away from Stephen's fictional situation toward an external matter, the claims made by certain live capitalists concerning the sanctity of their factories, as the parenthetical statement indicates. Stephen is almost forgotten as a character with established mannerisms and problems; the remark he does not make to Mrs. Pegler about "Divine Right" is put into (and then taken out of) his mouth by Dickens's narrator. The statement conveys a mordancy quite out of keeping with Stephen's character as it is presented elsewhere in the novel. Dickens is, of course, free to make Stephen a mouthpiece if he thinks such a move will advance the artistic effect he has in mind; but he is open to criticism on two fronts if, by doing so, he sacrifices an artistic effect (Stephen's consistency as a fictional character) for a polemical aside (". . . I have heard claims almost as magnificent of late years").

A similar parenthetical assertion appears in the description of Slackbridge's harangue:

> That every man felt his condition to be, somehow or other, worse than it might be; that every man considered it incumbent to join the rest

towards the making of it better; that every man felt his only hope to
be in his allying himself to the comrades by whom he was surrounded;
and that in this belief, right or wrong (unhappily wrong then), the
whole of that crowd were gravely, deeply, faithfully in earnest; must
have been as plain to any one who chose to see what was there, as the
bare beams of the roof and the whitened brick walls. (II, iv)

As David Lodge persuasively demonstrates in "The Rhetoric of
Hard Times," the *fictional* possibilities for good or evil inherent in
the United Aggregate Tribunal are but sketchily conveyed within
the novel. The narrator's assurance that the Coketown workers
were "unhappily wrong" in their impulse to unite assumes an *a
priori* conviction, shared by the readers, that real labor unions
are not the answer to England's real problems. Not every reader,
naturally enough, accepts this assessment of the situation as deno-
tatively true. By removing the issue from the sphere of the novel
and injecting it into the arena of public debate, Dickens again
encouraged readers to respond to *Hard Times* as argument rather
than fiction.

The passages just examined are isolated examples of Dickens's
divided loyalties to internal consistency and external denotation.
The uneasy coexistence of Dickens the novelist and Dickens the
propagandist is more pervasive than these examples alone indicate.
Stephen Blackpool's speech to Bounderby (II, v), quoted earlier,
bears all the signs of an authorially approved commentary on the
world of the novel. Much care is taken prior to this scene to invest
Stephen with humble but admirable qualities, and the contrast
between him and his bullying employer reinforces the positive
virtues that the narrator has previously ascribed to Stephen.
Nothing said in this speech is directly refuted in the novel, least of
all by Bounderby, who can only sputter at his employee's implacable
rightness. The scene is thus set for an exposition, by a sympathetic
and trustworthy character, of the values that ought to adhere in this
fictional world. But Stephen's speech is a much less convincing
argument for the feasibility of such values than it may seem at
first. His plea for humanity and love as the best remedy for Coketown's "muddle" appears to depend much less on what precedes
and follows this scene within the novel than on Dickens's private
beliefs concerning the likelihood of real social reforms. Stephen is
made to argue as if he had been called upon to transform English
society, not simply to provide an alternative to the fictional situation embodied in the world of *Hard Times*. Consequently, his

reply does not fully correspond to the fictional issues that make such a reply necessary. A reader is forced to assume that Dickens saw Stephen's answer as the "right" one for England's problems in the 1850's, but the right answer for England is not necessarily the right answer for the world of Coketown. This speech does, in fact, force Dickens into an impossible situation, one in which the demands of art and propaganda become patently contradictory. Within the novel, his artistic talents created, in Bounderby, a forceful portrait of a character incapable of change; yet his doubts about actually changing English industrial practices through agitation or new laws led him to assert that a change in Bounderby was the only solution to the fictional problems he had created. The impasse is clear: a radical alteration in Bounderby's character along the lines urged by Stephen would have seemed artistically unpremeditated, while Stephen's medicine for the disease of Coketown must seem artistically inefficacious. When Stephen's answer is tested within the world of the novel, it seems curiously "wrong" as a balm for his troubles. The one instance in which generosity is shown to Stephen by someone above him occurs when Louisa visits him after he has been fired by her husband; this instance, strangely enough, leads inexorably to Stephen's death. Louisa's humane gesture inspires Tom Gradgrind to implicate Blackpool in the planned robbery of Bounderby's bank. Stephen, of course, dies on his way back to Coketown to clear himself of that charge. The healing power of love and humanity between the classes is asserted in Stephen's speech and elsewhere in *Hard Times,* but this power is denied when it is embodied in a specific action.

If, as these introductory remarks suggest, *Hard Times* is a limited success, it is also an endlessly fascinating work, fascinating both despite and because of Dickens's ambivalence toward the demands of art and argument. The schoolroom scenes, the descriptions of Coketown, the hateful yet comic portrait of Bounderby, and the account of Mrs. Sparsit's frantic chase illustrate Dickens at his best; in these passages and scenes, the pressure of his language creates enduring images of locales, characters, and events, images that are liberated from the prosaic entailments of life and dependent on nothing but the genius of their maker:

> It had a black canal in it, and a river that ran purple with ill-smelling dye, and vast piles of building full of windows where there was a rattling and a trembling all day long, and where the piston of the steam engine worked monotonously up and down, like the head

of an elephant in a state of melancholy madness. It contained several
large streets all very like one another, and many small streets still
more like one another, inhabited by people equally like one another,
who all went in and out at the same hours, with the same sound upon
the same pavements, to do the same work, and to whom every day
was the same as yesterday and to-morrow, and every year the counterpart of the last and the next. (I, v)

The force of the diction and syntax in this passage is centripetal,
inward toward the creation of a landscape that needs no outside
referent to validate it. The language does not ask a reader to
believe that Coketown is Manchester, England; the repeated con-
nectives, the monotonously parallel clauses, the audacious steam
engine-elephant simile, all compel him to believe that *this* place is
a nightmare of threatening, inhuman force. It is left to the reader
to make an analogy between this nightmare and a real town he
might know of, or live in, or own.

Dickens did not always trust his readers to see such analogies for
themselves. He chose, instead, to make *Hard Times* dependent on
assertions of literal correspondence with the outside world; the
price he paid for this gesture was a surrendering of certain pre-
rogatives that he and his novel could have enjoyed. Until quite
recently, *Hard Times* has suffered from the absence of these pre-
rogatives. It has become increasingly evident, however, that this
novel raises vital questions concerning the relationship between
fictional worlds and the impressionistic, fragmented worlds that
men call real; it questions the power of art to change men and
societies and the propriety of art that attempts to do so. For those
interested in seeking answers to these questions, no better point
of origin for that quest can be found than the text of *Hard Times*.

Editor's Note

Credit for the resurgence of critical interest in *Hard Times*
during the past two decades belongs chiefly to F. R. Leavis, the
distinguished and provocative British critic. Leavis's article on
Hard Times, "The Novel as Dramatic Poem: 'Hard Times,'"
which first appeared in 1947, became the concluding chapter of his
The Great Tradition, an influential study of English fiction that
was published the following year. Leavis wrote of *Hard Times*:
". . . of all Dickens's works, it is the one that has all the strength

of his genius, together with a strength no other of them can show—
that of a completely serious work of art." [13] After twenty years of
renewed interest in this novel, Leavis's remarks seem less significant
than does the fact that he made them. Since *Hard Times* was then
one of Dickens's least-read novels, Leavis buttressed his argument
with extensive quotations; these passages could not be abridged
without weakening or misrepresenting his commentary, yet they
stretch his argument to a length unsuitable for inclusion in this
volume. In all fairness, Leavis's evaluation of *Hard Times* should
be placed in the context of *The Great Tradition*; his assessment
of that novel's "strength" is intimately related to the qualities of
"greatness" he postulates in earlier chapters of his study.

Also omitted from this selection are several articles that systemati-
cally take issue with Leavis's commendation of *Hard Times*. Another volume of this length could be compiled from entries
in the Leavis controversy;[14] it was felt that a severely abridged
presentation of this dispute would reflect unfairly the participants'
contributions, accentuate acrimony at the expense of information,
and unnecessarily limit the variety and scope of critical positions
set forth in this volume. The concluding footnote lists those
articles relevant to this dispute, and the "Selected Bibliography"
singles out several of particular merit.

[13] F. R. Leavis, *The Great Tradition* (New York: New York University Press
[paperback], 1963), p. 227.
[14] F. R. Leavis, "The Novel as Dramatic Poem: 'Hard Times,'" *Scrutiny*, XIV
(1947), 185–203, reprinted as "'Hard Times': An Analytic Note" in *The Great
Tradition* (London, 1948), pp. 227–48; A. J. A. Waldock, "The Status of *Hard
Times*," *Southerly*, IX (1948), 33–39; John Holloway, "*Hard Times*, a History
and a Criticism," in *Dickens and the Twentieth Century*, ed. John Gross and
Gabriel Pearson (London: Routledge & Kegan Paul Ltd.; Toronto: University
of Toronto Press, 1962), pp. 159–74; David Hirsch, "*Hard Times* and F. R.
Leavis," *Criticism*, VI (Winter, 1964), 1–16; John W. Gibson, "*Hard Times*:
A Further Note," *Dickens Studies*, I (1965), 90–101; Robin Gilmour, "The
Gradgrind School: Political Economy in the Classroom," *Victorian Studies*, XI
(December, 1967), 207–24.

PART ONE

Interpretations

The Battle for Preston

by K. J. Fielding

A hundred years ago England was becoming increasingly conscious of the strike as a means of forcible negotiation. In the City,
gentlemen had to walk when the cabbies objected to the new
Act reducing their fares to 6d. a mile; while, in Wigan, striking
miners attacked the Royal Hotel where their masters met, and
were scattered only by a detachment of the 34th Foot. Although
the nation was prosperous, the miners were out, the bricklayers
were out, and the engineers were back only after a determined
effort to gain effective power for their new Amalgamated Society.
The outbreaks were local; but they were evidence of general unrest.
When the weavers of Preston went on strike in October 1853,
therefore, the whole country was vitally interested in this new
challenge to the domination of the masters.

The history of such industrial disputes is often to be found in
newspapers rather than official records; but with the strike at
Preston it was taken up by novelists and special feature-writers as
well as by the daily press. Charles Dickens paid a visit in order to
write an article for *Household Words*; *The Leisure Hour* had a
special report entitled "A Town on Strike"; and "A Prestonian"
contributed a long analysis to *Eliza Cook's Journal*. No less informative were Dickens's *Hard Times* and Mrs. Gaskell's *North and
South*; for though they had not had the intention of taking the
disputes between Capital and Labour as their subject before the
Preston strike began, there is no doubt that it influenced them
strongly once they started to write.[1]

"The Battle for Preston" *by K. J. Fielding. From* The Dickensian, *L, part 4,
no. 312 (September, 1954), 159–62. Copyright © 1954 by K. J. Fielding. Reprinted
by permission of the author and The Dickens Fellowship.*

[1] *Hard Times* was published in *Household Words* from April 1st to August

The causes of the strike are not easy to define. In its simplest form it was a straightforward dispute about wages. But the negotiations were badly handled, and on both sides the issue soon became entirely a matter of principle, the men demanding a rise of "a whole ten per cent." and the masters refusing to be "coerced." When it was clear that the weavers would be able to force the mill-owners to agree one by one, by staging separate strikes against each employer in turn, the masters closed the mills. The men declared it a lock-out, and the mill-owners insisted it was a strike; but neither were prepared to surrender.

The situation was complicated by further differences, but those which were openly debated were less important than the fundamental struggle for power. For although they had no permanent union the strikers focussed the attention of the country on Preston, since if they won the same process could evidently be repeated elsewhere with the same effect.

The leaders of the strike seldom advanced their claims beyond the mere ten per cent., and it was largely the employers who saw it as a contest "not only of capital against labour but that of property against communism." This was the thesis of Henry Ashworth, a spokesman for the mill-owners at a meeting of the British Association at Liverpool. In Mrs. Gaskell's *North and South* the mill-owner's mother, Mrs. Thornton, expresses the same point of view equally strongly:

> "A strike?" asked Margaret. "What for? What are they going to strike for?"
> "For the mastership and ownership of other people's property," said Mrs. Thornton, with a fierce snort . . .
> "They are wanting higher wages, I suppose?" asked Mr. Hale.
> "That is the face of the thing. But the truth is, they want to be masters, and make the masters slaves on their own ground."

12th, and was followed by *North and South* from September 2nd, 1854, to January 27th, 1855. Mrs. Gaskell, however, had started before Dickens. After seeing part of the novel Forster [John Forster, Dickens's friend and biographer] had written to her on January 16th, 1854, "I say very heartily and earnestly go on with the story whether it be for Dickens or not"; and, on April 10th: "As to the current which Dickens's story is likely to take I have regretted to see that the manufacturing discontents are likely to clash with part of your plan, but . . . I *know* with what a different purpose and subsidiary to what quite opposite manifestations of character and passion *your* strike will be introduced, and I am your witness, if necessary, that your notion in this matter existed before and quite independently of his."—From transcripts (Shorter collection), Brotherton Library, University of Leeds.

Such was certainly the employers' view, and it was one with which Mrs. Gaskell, herself, generally agreed though she could not resist a touch of satire when it was expressed by the master's mother. When Mr. Hale asks Mr. Thornton, "Is there necessity for calling it *a battle* between two classes?" he sternly replies: "It is true." This was the reason why the masters refused to consent to arbitration, for it was they who openly recognised the dispute as a class struggle and who refused to allow themselves to be outflanked by outside interference. "We will hardly submit to the decision of an umpire," declares Thornton, "much less to the intervention of a meddler with only a smattering of the knowledge of the real facts of the case, even though that meddler be called the High Court of Parliament."

Public opinion did not question the right to strike, but deplored the serious losses caused by 20,000 workers being idle for nearly seven months. There was widespread sympathy for the weavers; and although it was recognised that the dispute could be decided only by arbitration or by the victory of either masters or men there was a general belief that such contests could be avoided in future if there were a better understanding between them. This opinion was most strongly voiced by Dickens in *Hard Times* and *Household Words*.

From the novel alone Dickens's opinions can easily be misunderstood, although in the article they had been much more openly expressed. With one eye on Cobden and Bright* he had concluded by asking:

> Gentlemen are found, in great manufacturing towns, ready enough to extol imbecile mediation with dangerous madmen abroad; can none be brought to think of authorised mediation and explanation at home? I do not suppose that such a knotted difficulty as this is to be at all untangled by a morning-party in the Adelphi; but . . . masters right, or men right . . . there is certain ruin to both in the continuance or frequent revival of this breach.

Dickens objected to the actual intransigence of the masters as strongly as he satirised the mill-owners in the novel, and though he made it clear that he thought the men were "engaged in an unreasonable struggle," he deplored the way in which even in the liberal press he had found "such references" to them "as might

* [Richard Cobden (1804–65) and John Bright (1811–88), spokesmen for the Utilitarian economics of the so-called Manchester School.]

have been made by an irascible General to rebels and brigands in arms." He maintained that there could be no permanent settlement by force, but only by conciliation.

In his own day Dickens was blamed for his portrait of the master, Josiah Bounderby, and more recently he has been condemned for his character of the trade union agitator Slackbridge, who has been dismissed as "a figment of his imagination." [2] Yet Mr. Humphry House has already pointed out, in *The Dickens World*, how Slackbridge was a development of "Gruffshaw," a delegate Dickens described in the article "On Strike"; and further enquiry now shows that "Gruffshaw" was a sketch of one of the actual strike leaders, Mortimer Grimshaw, whom Dickens heard addressing a meeting on his visit to Preston. An independent report by a local observer shows that his description was far from being exaggerated:

> Mortimer Grimshaw is a . . . man very much marked with the small-pox. He is well known by his white hat, which, I suppose, he wears after the fashion of Hunt and Cobbett . . . And, as John Bright plants his elevated fist firmly in advance, whilst eloquently expounding his doctrines of the Peace Society, so Mortimer Grimshaw advocates liberty to the oppressed "factory slaves" with a dogmatical invective and a blatant vituperation more worthy of a Russian despot than an English patriot.[3]

The real leader of the weavers was George Cowell, a man of great ability, good sense and moderation, and Dickens's chief inaccuracy was in writing of Slackbridge as if he were typical of the men's representatives. Yet both Grimshaw and Cowell were local men, unheard of before the strike, whereas Slackbridge is introduced as an outside agitator. The differences between the book and the article in *Household Words* are enough to show that such changes were deliberate, and from what is known of Dickens's intentions it is clear that he wanted to give it a rather wider significance. He had had the idea of the novel for some time, and in directing his satire against union officials rather than local strike leaders there is little doubt that he had in mind the strike of the Amalgamated Society of Engineers, which had centred on Manchester in 1851. Apart from Grimshaw, who was by no means typical, the strike leaders were careful in their activities; and, at one

[2] Edgar Johnson, *Charles Dickens, His Tragedy and Triumph* [New York], 1953, II, 811.

[3] "Lancashire Stump Oratory," *Eliza Cook's Journal*, August 19, 1854, p. 258.

of the first meetings after the lock-out George Cowell had even concluded by calling for three cheers for "Queen Victoria and the Royal Family," followed by three more for "Ten per cent. and the people."

The only danger to peace was in the introduction of blacklegs or "knobsticks," in order to work some of the mills which stayed open; but they were unmentioned by Dickens and other reporters, though they played an important part at Preston and were the cause of the riot in *North and South*. No doubt Mrs. Gaskell also had earlier strikes in mind, but the course of events she described in the novel was very close to what actually happened. Both in fact and fiction the masters imported a large body of Irish; but at Preston the leaders had a proper control over their supporters and violence was avoided. It was in trying to persuade some of the Irish to break their contracts, however, that several of the strike-leaders at Preston laid themselves open to prosecution. They were arrested, and released on bail; and it was only because the dispute came to an end that they were never brought to trial.

The end of the strike was brought about by a failure in funds, for the men had been maintained by adequate contributions collected from all the workers in the neighbouring textile towns. At the end of the fourth week the weavers were even jubilantly singing a broadside ballad which gave their employers "A Month's Notice":

> We've Blackburn at one side
>   And Stockport at the other,
> And we know they will stick true to us,
>   Like sister and like brother.
> And if they'll send us their support,
>   And never do lament,
> We'll stand out firmly side by side,
>   All for our ten per cent.[4]

But though all went well for the weavers as long as their fraternal comrades at Stockport and Blackburn were content to contribute sixpence a week to keep them out, at the critical moment their leaders lost control and the Stockport workers came out on a strike of their own. Neither district was able to support itself alone, and

[4] From an important, three-volume collection of cuttings, broadsides and pamphlets about the strike, now in the County Record Office, Preston.

after long months of living on strike pay it was disastrous at Preston. The contributions to the central fund dropped at once, the weavers began to go back, and by the beginning of May the strike was over in its twenty-ninth week. The public lost interest immediately, for a few days later Mr. Gladstone announced that a duty of a shilling a gallon was to be added to Scotch whisky and that the income tax was doubled. The mill chimneys began to smoke once more as another war began, and new orders were placed as troops were embarked for the Crimea.

Politics

by Humphry House

In all this work of the early 'fifties the idea of muddle is spreading over wider and wider social fields. *Hard Times* came out between April and August 1854, and Stephen Blackpool's reiterated comment, " 'Tis a' a muddle" is superficially the least hopeful moral to be got from any novel Dickens wrote. Discussion of the book has often centred too much on Macaulay's condemnation of it as "sullen socialism," and the almost exaggerated praise that Ruskin gave it in *Unto this Last*; for it is the least read of the novels and probably also the least enjoyed by those who read it. Even Mr. Edwin Pugh[1] called it "dry," "hard," and "the least alluring" of them all. The most common general explanation of the book's failure is that Dickens was writing of people and things quite outside the range of his own experience. This is, in itself, of course, no explanation at all, or *A Tale of Two Cities* would stand equally condemned; but the decision to write just when he did about industrial Lancashire with no more experience than deliberate copy-hunting could give him was peculiar in several ways. The fashion for industrial novels was already passing: *Martin Armstrong, Helen Fleetwood, Sybil, Mary Barton,*[2] and forgotten stories by such people as Camilla Toulmin, belong to the late 'thirties and 'forties, the period of Chartism, terrific unemployment and angry strikes. The

From "Politics." *From* The Dickens World *by Humphry House (London: Oxford University Press, 1941), pp. 203–11. Reprinted by permission of the publisher. [This selection is taken from a broader discussion of the political influences that operated on Dickens the novelist.]*

[1] [Edwin Pugh (1874–1930), prolific novelist and essayist, author of *The Charles Dickens Originals* (London, 1912).]

[2] [*Michael Armstrong, the Factory Boy* (1840), here mistitled "*Martin Armstrong,*" by Mrs. Frances Trollope (1780–1863); *Helen Fleetwood* (1841) by Mrs. Charlotte Elizabeth Tonna (1790–1846); *Sybil* (1845) by Benjamin Disraeli (1804–81); *Mary Barton* (1848) by Mrs. Elizabeth Cleghorn Gaskell (1810–65).]

experience and motives behind their authors were very various. Mrs. Trollope, who had to write for money and had made her name with social criticism, found a topical subject and approached it with an average sense of decency and justice; Mrs. Tonna was inspired by her evangelical faith to a hatred of the factory system and its child employment even more passionate than Ashley's,[3] Disraeli was caught for a moment by an image of feudalism and found his experience in official reports; Mrs. Gaskell lived every day among the things she wrote of, and only discovered her talent because she thought the experience had to be used.

It has often been said that Dickens was a good deal influenced by *Mary Barton* in writing *Hard Times*: it might even be added that he was influenced by Elizabeth Gaskell herself [4]—it is impossible that he should have known her without being half in love—for his editorial letters about her work show an affectionate care abnormal even for him. But there was never any question of a conscious and deliberate imitation of her, or of Carlyle, or of anybody else. The strange thing is that though most readers find *Hard Times* dry and brain-spun, Dickens said of it himself that he had not meant to write a new story for a year, when the idea laid hold of him by the throat in a very violent manner.

What this central idea was there is no means of knowing; but it is plain that *Hard Times* is one of Dickens's most thought-about books. One of the reasons why, in the 'fifties, his novels begin to show a greater complication of plot than before, is that he was intending to use them as a vehicle of more concentrated sociological argument. All his journalism shows too that he was *thinking* much more about social problems, whereas earlier he had been content to feel mainly, and to record a thought, when it occurred, in emotional dress. The objection to such a character as Gradgrind is not just that he is a burlesque and an exaggeration—so are Squeers and Pecksniff—but rather that in him the satire is directed against a kind of thought: he is in fact the only major Dickens character who is meant to be an "intellectual": "His character was not unkind, all things considered; it might have been a very kind one indeed if he had only made some round mistake in the arithmetic that balanced it, years ago." Dickens was caught with the

[3] [Anthony Ashley Cooper, 7th Earl of Shaftesbury (1801–85), member of Parliament and militant champion of the rights of British workers.]
[4] From his letter of April 21, 1854, it is plain that he had talked over the story with her in some detail when he was in the North.

idea of a man living by a certain philosophy, as in the past he had
often been caught with the idea of a man living by a master vice
such as miserhood or hypocrisy or pride. Such vices he understood,
but he did not understand enough of any philosophy even to be
able to guy it successfully. But he obviously felt during the 'fifties,
when Public Health and Administrative Reform were keeping him
so closely to social-political problems, that there must be some
essential flaw in the reasoning of such a man as Bright. The creation
of Gradgrind is an attempt to track it down. The despondent
atmosphere of the whole book reflects the failure to do so.

This atmosphere is concentrated in Stephen Blackpool. In him
Dickens tried to rescue the idea of personality in an individual industrial worker. Stephen's successive defeats by the Law, by the
Trade Union, and by his employer might have become the material
of genuine tragedy, if Dickens had been prepared to accept his
death from the beginning as inevitable and unanswerable; but he
was hankering all the time after a way to avoid the proper tragic
solution, and the result is nothing but a slow record of inglorious
misery and defeat. Dickens did not want to admit that Stephen's
bargaining power—whether against Bounderby, his marriage, or
life itself—was negligible, but wrote as if there might be an unexpected solution at every turn. There is no difficulty about Stephen's
relation to the Law or about his relation to Bounderby;[5] the true
crux is in the part of the plot that deals with the Trade Union, and
in making it so Dickens was apparently trying to work out, in the
actual writing of the book, the implications of his old ideal of *man
to man* benevolence in the relations between employers and labour
in large-scale industry. Three points were emphasized in the treatment of the Union—Stephen's inexplicable obstinacy in refusing to

[5] [John] Ruskin's judgment that Bounderby was merely a "dramatic monster,
instead of a characteristic example of a worldly master" is probably more or
less true if we assume Coketown to be Manchester and Bounderby a man of
the local prominence that Dickens gives him. But if Coketown was some smaller
place, a monster of that kind might well have got such power over its life.
Mr. and Mrs. Hammond have, for instance, found a possible original (*Town
Labourer,* p. 302): "P———d, the Beggar-maker, who sits on the destinies of the
Poor, we have made a Man of him, whose Mother hawked about the streets
a small Basket; on two Spinners being deputed to ask for a small advance of
Price, had the audacity to thrust one of them from him with an Umbrella and
discharged them both" (Letter from Committee of Manchester Weavers, 1823,
Home Office Papers, 40, p. 18). Such a man might well have grown into
Bounderby by the 'fifties.

join it; Dickens's hatred of Slackbridge; and the difference of mood and attitude of the other workers towards Stephen as men and as Union members under Slackbridge's influence.

For the Union meeting itself he did a thing which was very rare for him—he deliberately went in search of copy, to Preston, to watch the effects of a strike of the cotton workers there which had dragged on for weeks. He seems to have gone expecting to find discontent, disorder, and even rioting, and his first impression caused surprise and a sort of sentimental gladness that everything was so quiet and the men generally so well-behaved. When he came to write up the visit for the article *On Strike* in *Household Words* (Feb. 11, 1854) there was overlaid upon this first impression a certain horror at the idleness. He seemed to be asking whether these were perhaps after all the lazy poor, in whose existence he had never believed. The article describes the two meetings of the strikers that he attended, and they are obviously the foundation for the Union meeting in *Hard Times*: it stresses their order and courtesy, the efficiency of the business and the competence of the men's local leaders; it decries the influence of an outside orator who is a prototype of Slackbridge; it makes clear that the men fully believed in the justice of their case, but that, at the same time, they had no hatred or resentment for most of the employers: it does, however, quote one example of a threatening notice against a particular man, together with various other placards and verses: the moral approval seems to be all on the side of the strikers. But the political conclusion is not that the strike is right:

> In any aspect in which it can be viewed, this strike and lock-out is a deplorable calamity. In its waste of time, in its waste of a great people's energy, in its waste of wages, in its waste of wealth that seeks to be employed, in its encroachment on the means of many thousands who are laboring from day to day, in the gulf of separation it hourly deepens between those whose interests must be understood to be identical or must be destroyed, it is a great national affliction. But, at this pass, anger is of no use, starving out is of no use—for what will that do, five years hence, but overshadow all the mills in England with the growth of a bitter remembrance?—political economy is a mere skeleton unless it has little human covering and filling out, a little human bloom upon it, and a little human warmth in it.

The only practical suggestion is that the dispute should be submitted immediately to impartial arbitrators agreed upon by both sides. This paragraph is extremely important and interesting, because in it Dickens accepts the fundamental ethical and political proposition of the political economy he generally so much deplores. The interests of employers and employed must be assumed to be identical or must be destroyed. The doctrine of the identity of interests was common to the utilitarians and the economists: on the question of *theory* there is no real difference between Dickens and W. R. Greg:[6] he is not in the least a Socialist.

This paragraph also helps to explain why the satire of Mr. Gradgrind is comparatively ineffective; for Dickens is not even intending to attack the whole philosophy which he thought was represented in the Manchester men; he is only attacking the excessive emphasis on statistics; in fact he is repeating Mr. Filer over again, and he seems to have no uneasiness about whether such satire is adequate or important. He is through all these years, however, extremely uneasy is his attempts to find a channel through which the desires and needs of an ordinary decent working man like Blackpool can find expression. Why, when he recognized the capacity of such men for conducting their own business, did he reject the Trade Union solution, and reject it as emphatically as a Manchester man like Greg?

On the whole the "Combinations" of the 'thirties and 'forties, whether organized locally, by trades, or nationally, had avowed revolutionary aims. The extent to which their members advocated the use of physical force was less important than the fact that they were widely believed to do so; but, physical force aside, they were revolutionary in the sense that they did not accept the doctrine of the natural identity of interests between Capital and Labour, and were in their political activities more or less conscious of a class-struggle; and this consciousness was shared by their opponents. The Chartist failure of '48 meant widespread disillusionment in the possibilities of working-class political action, and the reviving unions of the 'fifties concentrated more on the immediate problem of collective bargaining within particular trades than on the for-

---

[6] [William Rathbone Greg (1809–91), essayist and conservative economist.] See especially Greg's long review of *Mary Barton*, of 1849, reprinted in *Mistaken Aims and Attainable Ideals of the Artizan Class* (1876) and his *English Socialism* of 1850. Both essays are directed against the impatient philanthropy of "feeling" as compared with the long-distance philanthropy of the economists. The cures for labour disputes are that the working class should be more provident and should, by the study of political economy, realize the necessary identity of their interests with those of the employers.

mation of huge amalgamations with political aims⁷ Dickens seems
to have realized that this change was happening, but he shared
two common popular misconceptions about it; the first was that the
leaders of such unions were bound to be demagogic frauds like
Gruffshaw and Slackbridge; and the second was that the unions
were likely to violate liberty by being exclusive and tyrannical
towards workers who refused to join them:⁸ both points were
heavily underlined in *Hard Times.* The first of these objections was
a legacy from the earlier amalgamating, revolutionary period, and
was very largely justified. For in the period of Chartism and the
large national unions the working-class movement was grotesquely
top-heavy and therefore unstable: the middle-class mistrust of
"demagogues" and "paid agitators," whatever its motives may have
been, was justified in the sense that national leadership had not
developed out of solidly organized cells of local opinion. Local
organization even in the 'fifties was likely, as in the Preston strike,
to be an *ad hoc* affair called into being by a particular dispute;
and Dickens was faithful in his reporting, in *On Strike,* of the way
that outside influence was likely to be overridden: but in *Hard
Times* he regarded local opinion as dynamically inferior to Slackbridge's bluster: he meant to imply that Stephen was socially boycotted in spite of a predominating feeling in his favour, and the
other workers bamboozled out of their better selves; and he made
the distortion seem more serious by giving Stephen no better reason
for not joining them than a mysterious promise. The objection to
unions on the ground of exclusiveness and tyranny followed inevitably from the general misunderstanding of their nature: Dickens
realized that when Stephen had been both boycotted by his fellow-
workers and sacked by Bounderby he had no chance of getting
another job; but he did not draw from this the conclusion that an
individual worker *cannot* be the equal of an employer in bargaining
power, and that the ideal bargaining for labour-price talked of by
the economists only had any meaning when the bargaining was
done by a unanimous combination. His emotional admiration for

⁷ The Amalgamated Society of Engineers, for instance, was founded in 1851,
and played a very important part in the development of Unionism in the next
twenty years.
⁸ Even [Charles] Kingsley, when calling himself a Socialist, wrote to a Manchester friend, March 28, 1856: "I admire your boldness in lifting up your
voices to expose the tyranny of 'Union' Strikes. From my own experience of
demagogues . . . I can well believe every word you say as to the 'humbug' connected with the inner working of them."

the conscientious blackleg was not based on any alternative argument. But he did not abandon all hope of finding some means other than the unions by which such men as Stephen might be politically and socially articulate; he was still groping after it later in the year in the address *To Working Men* and the other articles on Public Health we have already discussed.

However, the failure of *Hard Times* in two main strands of its plot and in so many of its major characters does not lessen the force of the mixture of fascination and repulsion that Dickens felt for the industrial scene in which the book was set. The fascination, which appears in the descriptions of the night railway journey out from Coketown to Bounderby's house, of the people surging to the mills in the morning, and returning at night to their various homes, has the interest in life and movement, which is plain everywhere in his work, heightened by greater speed and tension. The repulsion is generally more marked, as it is in the Black Country parts of *The Old Curiosity Shop*; the dismal appearance of the competing chapels, the rigidity of the Bounderby bank and the grim business discipline which intrudes on every detail even of domestic life, express once more the Southerner's dismay at what he could not assimilate; but underlying it there is unresting indignation at the impoverishment of human life that such things implied. This indignation is not crude and immature anger, but rather a disturbed mood that colours every perception, contributing a great deal to the unpopularity of *Hard Times*. The book is ultimately unsatisfying and oddly uncomfortable to nearly all its readers; but this very fact is the main thing that has to be considered in assessing its value as a novel; unanswerable disquiet was normal among the very few who were not misled into the easy optimism in which Bagehot[9] typifies the 'fifties; Ruskin's exaggerated praise of *Hard Times* may be understood as a recognition that a work of art, by conveying this at least to others, might make up for many other imperfections; and even those writers whose economics and social criticism were more solid and thoughtful than Dickens's betray in their own ways shifting of opinion and misplacement of emphasis—Mill, Ruskin, and Arnold are examples—which equally, express the practical embarrassment of the time.

[9] [Walter Bagehot (1826–1877), prominent social and literary critic.]

Good Intentions and Bad Results

by Philip Collins

Hard Times began to appear in *Household Words* on 1 April 1854. Dickens had been thinking about it since the previous autumn, and his cogitations begin to appear in his letters in January 1854. At the end of that month he visited Preston, to get material for the industrial and trade-union aspects of the novel; a few weeks later he began to collect circus-slang; and on 25 January he had written to Wills: "I want (for the story I am trying to hammer out) the Educational Board's series of questions for the examination of *teachers* in schools. Will you get it?" [1]

At the beginning of the novel, Mr. M'Choakumchild is just about to give his first lesson. He has just qualified at a training college, so he belongs to a generation which had lately been receiving a good deal of attention. The first batch of Queen's Scholars, enlisted as pupil-teachers under Kay-Shuttleworth's 1846 Minutes, had emerged from the training colleges in 1853, and naturally their graduation and departure to the schools had renewed popular interest in the scheme. Much had been promised from it: now its results could be seen and judged. Dickens would doubtless be particularly interested to read accounts of these new certificated teachers, for he had long been urging that unqualified teachers should be eliminated.[2] It is, however, typical of his outlook and technique

---

From "Good Intentions and Bad Results." *From* Dickens and Education *by Philip Collins (London: Macmillan & Co. Ltd.; New York: St. Martin's Press, Inc.; Toronto: The Macmillan Co. of Canada, Ltd., 1963), pp. 148–55. Copyright © 1963 by Philip Collins. Reprinted by permission of the publishers. [In the chapter from which this essay is taken, the author discusses the teachers, good and bad, who appear in Dickens's novels.]*

[1] [Letter from] Dickens to [W. H.] Wills, 25 January 1854 (Huntington Library MSS).

[2] See above, pp. 92–97, 123, 138. [The author here refers the reader to earlier passages in his book that describe Dickens's concern with educational malpractices.]

that he presents M'Choakumchild and his training entirely from
a satirical point of view:

He and some one hundred and forty other schoolmasters, had been
lately turned at the same time, in the same factory, on the same
principles, like so many pianoforte legs. He had been put through
an immense variety of paces, and had answered volumes of head-
breaking questions. Orthography, etymology, syntax, and prosody,
biography, astronomy, geography, and general cosmography, the
sciences of compound proportion, algebra, land-surveying and levelling, vocal music, and drawing from models, were all at the ends of
his ten chilled fingers. He had worked his stony way into Her
Majesty's most Honourable Privy Council's Schedule B, and had
taken the bloom off the higher branches of mathematics and physical
science, French, German, Latin and Greek. He knew all about all the
Water Sheds of all the world (whatever they are), and all the histories
of all the peoples, and all the names of all the rivers and mountains,
and all the productions, manners, and customs of all the countries,
and all their boundaries and bearings on the two-and-thirty points of
the compass. Ah, rather overdone, M'Choakumchild. If he had only
learnt a little less, how infinitely better he might have taught much
more! [3]

Mr. M'Choakumchild is explicitly enough said to be representative, and in various respects he is so. Thus, he is assisted in the
school by his wife; this was the ideal standard pattern of the period.
The Scottish prefix to his name is, perhaps, a reference to the fact
that England at that time imported large numbers of trained
teachers from Scotland, or it may be a way of associating him and
his educational ideas with the "Scotch Feeloosofers" and economists
identified in the public mind with the hard-headed utilitarianism
being attacked in *Hard Times*. Dickens certainly thought well of
his criticisms of the training college regime, for he virtually repeated
them ten years later when describing Bradley Headstone (the *stone*
of whose name also links him to the *hard* of *Hard Times*).

He had acquired mechanically a great store of teacher's knowledge.
He could do mental arithmetic mechanically, sing at sight mechanically, blow various wind instruments mechanically, even play the
great church organ mechanically. From his early childhood up, his
mind had been a place of mechanical stowage. The arrangement of
his wholesale warehouse, so that it might be always ready to meet

---

[3] *HT*, I, ii, 8. [The edition of *Hard Times* cited here and in future references
to the novel in this essay is that in the *New Oxford Illustrated Dickens* (1947–
58).]

the demands of retail dealers—history here, geography there, astronomy to the right, political economy to the left—natural history, the physical sciences, figures, music, the lower mathematics, and what not, all in their several places—his care had imparted to his countenance a look of care; while the habit of questioning and being questioned had given him a suspicious manner, or a manner that would be better described as one of lying in wait. . . . He always seemed to be uneasy lest anything should be missing from his mental warehouse, and taking stock to assure himself.[4]

The intellectual insecurity of Headstone ("a kind of settled trouble in the face") replaces the relentless confidence of M'Choakumchild, and is connected with the social unease which provides the new theme in this later study of the new-style schoolmaster.

When *Hard Times* was published, a teachers' magazine reprinted without comment the paragraph about M'Choakumchild, under the title "Description of a Modern Trained and Certificated Schoolmaster." Later, a correspondent protested that it was no disadvantage for M'Choakumchild to know so much, provided that he was "apt to teach." The *Westminster,* reviewing the novel, noted with disappointment that the industrial theme, Dickens's treatment of which had been eagerly awaited, had been "subordinated and made incidental" to the educational one, and it maintained that Dickens's satire was directed against a system which "we are not aware of . . . being in operation anywhere in England. . . . If there are Gradgrind schools, they are not sufficiently numerous to be generally known." [5] Dickens was, of course, using these opening school chapters to express not only his criticisms of some educational practices but also the larger themes of the book: but how just was his satire on the training colleges, and on the teaching methods they encouraged or tolerated?

About the training colleges, certainly, the disquiet that Dickens expresses here was widespread both among laymen and professionals—Her Majesty's Inspectors, headmasters, and some principals of the colleges themselves. In the same year as *Hard Times,* Jelinger Symons, HMI, noted that "a very widely-spread notion prevails, entertained by various ranks of persons," that the teaching in schools was too little adapted to the real needs and capacities of the children. He agreed, and said that he was very tolerant of schools which succeeded in giving some useful practical instruction,

---

[4] *OMF,* II, i, 217. [*Our Mutual Friend* in the New *Oxford Illustrated Dickens.*]
[5] *The School and the Teacher,* I, May and June 1854, 95, 116; *Westminster Review,* NS VI, October 1854, 605.

even if their pupils remained ignorant of "the chronology of the
kings of Israel and . . . the tributaries of the Euphrates, and had
never heard of Agamemnon." He deplored "those mechanical mock-
eries of education" which were still too common, concentrating on
the mind and memory instead of developing "the whole child."
A few years later, the Newcastle Commission (appointed in 1858
"to inquire into the Present State of Popular Education in England") heard much evidence to the same effect. One training college principal criticised the conditions under which the colleges
had to operate, in terms very similar to Dickens's.

> Let us look at the programme of subjects required to be known by
> the students. Their character and their number at once indicate that
> the present course pursued in training schools tends to *impart infor-
> mation* rather than to *develope the faculties and to discipline the
> mind*. Vast demands are made on the memory, little is done for the
> improvement of the judgment or reasoning powers. . . . To use a
> very significant and very intelligible expression, the great feature of
> the course of study pursued in training colleges is *cram*. In such sub-
> jects as Old Testament history, Church history, outlines of English
> history, there is necessarily an immense preponderance of names,
> dates, and facts, which have to be *remembered* but not *digested*.

The students therefore left college, he alleged, "with *full* but comparatively *languid* and *unbraced* minds." Many other witnesses
gave similar evidence. A headmaster complained that the colleges
neither trained their pupils' intellects nor taught them how to
teach: instead, the stress was on "scholarship"—"I mean a little
trigonometry,—a little acquaintance with Latin,—a little informa-
tion in that way; smallware scholarship, if I may say so without
impropriety." One Inspector, echoing Dickens, had suggested to
the Newcastle Commission that "it would be far better if you
could get schoolmasters with less knowledge and more education."
A student never had time to think about the facts learned at college,
said another witness—"and, in very many instances, he or she does
nothing more than 'flower' at the time of the examination, and
degenerate continuously afterwards." [6] This had long been a com-

[6] Symons, "On Industrial Schools," in *Lectures in Connection with the Educational Exhibition at St. Martin's Hall* [London], 1854, 87–89; Rev. H. G. Robin-
son, Principal of York Training College, *Newcastle Commission* [London, 1861],
IV, 404; W. A. Shields, Master of the Peckham Birkbeck School, *ibid.*, VI, 543;
Rev. J. W. Blakesley, formerly Tutor of Trinity College, Cambridge, *ibid.*, V,
89.

plaint in the Annual Reports of many of the Inspectors. Matthew
Arnold, for instance, often wrote in this strain, and—to quote just
one other instance—one of his colleagues reported on pupil-teachers
in 1856, that they received an immense amount of crude, undigested
facts without learning to think or to express themselves—"They
become overlaid with facts. Playing upon the surface of many
objects, and mastering none, their memory is unwholesomely stimu-
lated, their judgment stunted and baffled." [7]

Recent historians of the training colleges and of the Inspectorate
have confirmed the judgments of these observers, and of Dickens.
This was a period, says Dr. Rich, when "The well-informed was too
often looked upon as the well-educated. . . . This confusion between information and education lay like a blight on the training
college world." He quotes typical teachers' *Manuals* of the 'fifties,
which instruct the aspiring teacher to "learn by heart facts of
Physical and Political Geography," and so on.[8] Another recent his-
torian sums up popular feeling about the training colleges, in terms
which show how representative Dickens was, both in his substantial
accuracy and in his prejudices:

> The fifties were a time of reaction against mechanical instruction,
> and oral teaching flourished. Many people, some through sheer
> prejudice, others, like a few of the inspectors, through genuine ap-
> prehension, thought the reaction was going too far. The former type
> generally argued that the new teachers were taught too much, that
> they could not come down to the level of the pupil, that they were
> discontented with their lot and aimed at taking Holy Orders. . . .
> As time went on, warnings against the injudicious teaching of too
> many subjects became more frequent, and some inspectors were
> inclined to support the popular notion that the trained teachers
> were being taught too much—a notion encouraged by the publication
> of the stiff examinations set at the training colleges.[9]

[7] *Minutes [of the Committee of Council on Education], 1856–7,* and Temple's
evidence to the Newcastle Commission, quoted by [R. W.] Rich, *Training of
Teachers [in England and Wales during the Nineteenth Century* (Cambridge,
1933)], 141, 154; cf. [Matthew] Arnold, *Reports [on Elementary Schools, 1852–
1882,* ed. Francis Sanford (London, 1889)], 19–20, 55–56, 94–95, 255–56.
[8] Rich, 150, 145. Dr. Gustav Ögren, in his *Trends in English Teachers' Training from 1800* (Stockholm, 1953), comes to similar conclusions.
[9] John Leese, *Personalities and Powers in English Education* [London], 1950,
60, 71. See also the comments of Nassau Senior on a specimen examination-
paper for teachers, and his protest against this fact-ridden training, in his
Suggestions [on Popular Education (London, 1861)], Chapter VIII ("Rendering
the Education in Public Schools more Practical and Elementary, and less En-

Popular feeling about the training colleges' curriculum was, then, based on some sound objections. They attempted to do too much, too fast: and there was a mechanical factory-like aridity in too many of them, symbolised by their buildings—as one principal put it, "the bald utilities and whitewashed parallelograms which have sometimes been set forth as a model." [10] There were, however, less worthy motives behind the common criticisms of the new trained teachers—a Philistine contempt for the "useless" subjects they had learned, and social snobbery against these half-educated upstarts. As will appear in my discussion of *Our Mutual Friend,* Dickens was not immune to the latter prejudice. He shows little sympathy, let alone admiration, for the ambitions of the new schoolteachers—neither their anxiety to achieve professional competence nor their understandable demand for better social recognition. In his book on the teaching profession, Dr. Asher Tropp argues that M'Choakumchild is not a true picture of the college-trained teacher of the period, though "there is some little truth" in the description. He offers a more sympathetic account of the background to the difficulties of M'Choakumchild and his like:

> . . . one cannot begin to understand the teachers of the period from 1846 to 1862 unless one realises their almost fierce desire to acquire knowledge. This knowledge may have lacked depth. . . . It was impossible to expect a high proportion of "cultured" teachers from pupil-teacherdom with its one-and-a-half hours of instruction a day. . . . The large number of teachers who did succeed in educating themselves, in the full sense of the word, is a tribute not to the pupil-teacher system but to the pupil-teachers and teachers themselves. . . . [But] the "stereotype" of the over-educated, conceited, ambitious teacher was very strong among the middle classes of this period.

Dickens adopts an external and a middle-class view of the situation. While regarding with some distaste the products of the system, he does not seek to understand the motives—personal and institutional, and many of them excellent—which had led to these unsatisfactory results. He does not, however, go to the silly extreme of Kingsley, who expresses this widespread prejudice with characteris-

cumbered by Biblical, Historical, and Geographical Facts, Dates, Figures, and Details").

[10] Derwent Coleridge, *The Teachers of the People* (1862), 33 (quoted by Rich, 88).

tic trenchancy. "There was a new schoolmistress in Vendale," he writes in *The Water Babies*: and he adds, "we will hope that she was not certificated." [11]

Though *Hard Times* starts in a school and is much concerned, implicitly, with educational issues, only the first two brief chapters actually take place in the schoolroom. M'Choakumchild never appears again, but there are a few references to him: Sissy Jupe tells Louisa Gradgrind about her mistakes in Political Economy lessons —she unfortunately believes that its first principle is "To do unto others as I would that they should do unto me," and she cannot properly distinguish between Natural Prosperity and National Prosperity nor between statistics and stutterings. [12] At the end of Chapter II, Mr. M'Choakumchild is about to give a lesson, but we do not stay to hear it; the only school activities we witness are Gradgrind's address on Facts and his interrogation of the class, and the talk given by the unnamed "Government officer" about the principles of Taste. What were Dickens's objects in devising these lessons, and how just are they as comments on the teaching-methods of the period?

Mr. Gradgrind's questions are a parody of the object-lesson, and Dickens's satire has the same qualities as were apparent in the passage about training colleges—a substantial accuracy, and a lack of curiosity about causes. Gradgrind has discovered that the father of the new girl present, Sissy Jupe, belongs to the horse-riding in Sleary's circus. To give a utilitarian respectability to this disgraceful circus job, he redefines Signor Jupe's occupation as "a veterinary surgeon, a farrier, and horsebreaker," and he also gives Sissy a new name—"Girl number twenty"—to accord with the impersonality of her new school. He then improves the occasion by asking Sissy to define a horse. She is flummoxed by this question, which is promptly answered by the inhuman prize-pupil Bitzer:

"Quadruped. Graminivorous. Forty teeth, namely twenty-four grinders, four eye-teeth, and twelve incisive. Sheds coat in the spring; in marshy countries, sheds hoofs, too. Hoofs hard, but requiring to be shod with iron. Age known by marks in mouth." Thus (and much more) Bitzer.

[11] [Asher] Tropp, *The School Teachers* [London, 1957], 24 and note; Charles Kingsley, *The Water Babies* (1863), end of Chapter II.
[12] *HT*, I, ix, 55–57.

"Now girl number twenty," said Mr. Gradgrind. "You know what a horse is." [13]

Mr. Gradgrind's superb reproof to the circus-girl caps this ludicrous episode, which introduces one of the major themes of the novel—the contrast between verbalised head-knowledge and the knowledge of the senses and the heart. The episode is also a fair comment on the contemporary passion for such definitions. Bitzer's mouthful could have come from any textbook or teachers' manual. To quote an example, the Notes for one Model-lesson begin with the delightful instruction, "Produce, draw, or imagine a cat"; the teacher should then ask some questions and give some facts about cats.

> Having proceeded thus far, determine the family Felinae, Lat. *felis*, English, feline. Synopsis of Felinae.—Front teeth in each jaw, 6; canine teeth, 2 in each jaw, very powerful and formed for tearing; molar or cheek teeth, 4 . . . [etc.]. Head, large and round; eyes . . . ; tongue. . . . Feet formed for walking; toes on the fore feet, 5;—hind feet, 4. . . .

Thus (and much more) *The School and the Teacher*. The only feature Dickens has omitted, to catch completely the spirit of these definitions, is this typical concern with Etymology. Another set of Notes in the same publication begins a lesson on Money with a fine specimen: "*Etymology.*—Money is so called because it was first made at the Temple of Juno Moneta. Here notice the peculiar name of the temple, its site, and a few interesting facts about such buildings." [14] Bitzer could doubtless have reeled off the roots of *quadruped* and *graminivorous*. One source of this current enthusiasm for such verbalisations, irrelevant and incomprehensible though they were to most pupils, was the hope of increasing the self-respect of teacher and child by a frequent reference to the Latin language and to ancient civilisation. These were valued culture-tokens, and teachers and training colleges had a pathetic belief in their efficacy for raising the tone of the profession.

The main intellectual ancestry of the "definition of a horse" has been excellently traced by Dr. John Manning. Dickens's parody was, he notes, used by an educationist at the time, to illustrate his objections to the Home and Colonial School Society's system of "object-lessons"—a system derived from Pestalozzi, who had devised this technique to encourage children to observe accurately, analyse,

[13] I, ii, 5.
[14] *The School and the Teacher*, IV (1857), 100–101, 11.

and correctly describe various natural phenomena. But the original idea soon became perverted—as appears in that instruction, "Produce, draw, or imagine a cat." Too often the children did not have in front of them the "object" under discussion, but only a blackboard or a mental picture, and the teacher began to take over from the children the analysis of its qualities, which were dictated in the familiar scientific-Latinate vocabulary. Dr. Manning quotes a report that little children, not two weeks in school, were "taught that certain parts of a sheep (or the picture of a sheep) are 'principal,' others 'secondary.' . . . One hears from infant mouths such terms as 'graminivorous and chalybeate, iridescent and amorphous, serrated and folliaceous, imbricated and indigenous.' " [15]

[15] John Manning, "Charles Dickens and the Oswego System," *Journal of the History of Ideas,* XVIII (1957), 580–83 (and cf. his *Dickens on Education* [Toronto and Oxford, 1959], 130–31).

Hard Times: The Problems of a
Weekly Serial

by John Butt and Kathleen Tillotson

Household Words had been running for some eighteen months when *Bleak House* was completed at the end of August 1853. While Dickens was engaged with his book he had no time to write anything for his magazine more substantial than articles; but once the book was out of the way, he could listen to the persuasions of Forster, Bradbury and Evans, and Wills. "There is such a fixed idea on the part of my printers and copartners in *Household Words,* that a story of me, continued from week to week, would make some unheard of effect with it that I am going to write one"; so he told Miss Coutts on 23 January 1854.[1] The decision had been taken some time earlier, however. On 20 January he sent Forster a list of fourteen titles for "the *Household Words* story," begging him to look at them "between this and two o'clock or so, when I will call. It is my usual day, you observe, on which I have jotted them down —Friday! It seems to me that there are three very good ones among them. I should like to know whether you hit upon the same."[2] Though he had not yet set himself to write, it would seem that he had already discussed the theme of the novel with Forster; for if he had not, he could scarcely have expected Forster to choose between titles for a single story so strictly committing as these: *According to Cocker, Prove it, Stubborn Things, Mr. Gradgrind's*

From "Hard Times: The Problems of a Weekly Serial." *From* Dickens at Work *by John Butt and Kathleen Tillotson (New York: Oxford University Press; London: Methuen and Co., Ltd., 1958), pp. 201–9. Reprinted by permission of the publishers.* [*In the second half of this essay, here omitted, the authors concentrate on Dickens's "number plans" for the final twelve weekly installments of* Hard Times.]

[1] [*The*] Letters [*of Charles Dickens,* ed. Walter Dexter (London, 1938)], II, 537.
[2] *Ibid.*

Facts, The Grindstone, Hard Times, Two and Two are Four, Something Tangible, Our Hardheaded Friend, Rust and Dust, Simple Arithmetic, A Matter of Calculation, A Mere Question of Figures, The Gradgrind Philosophy.

These rejected titles and those in the manuscript—*Fact, Hardheaded Gradgrind, Hard Heads and Soft Hearts, Heads and Tales, Black and White*—remain of interest, since they seem to indicate the limits within which the book would move. The irony implicit in *Something Tangible, A Matter of Calculation,* and *A Mere Question of Figures* suggests that the novel will open up areas of experience beyond the reach of Mr. Gradgrind's philosophy, and the importance of feelings, disregarded by the political economists, is represented in *Hard Heads and Soft Hearts,* while *Heads and Tales* seems to forecast the opposition of fact and fancy so prominent in the scenes at Sleary's Circus troupe. These titles show that the story would appropriately appear in the columns of *Household Words,* whose policy Dickens had defined in an initial address (30 March 1850):

. . . No more utilitarian spirit, no iron binding of the mind to grim realities, will give a harsh tone to our *Household Words.* In the bosoms of the young and old, of the well-to-do and of the poor, we would tenderly cherish that light of Fancy which is inherent in the human breast; which, according to its nurture, burns with an inspiring flame, or sinks into a sullen glare, but which (or woe betide that day!) can never be extinguished.

The same day on which he consulted Forster about the title, Dickens sat down to plan the book. On a sheet of paper preserved in the manuscript he wrote first the date and then a memorandum on quantity, which reads as follows:

One sheet (16 pages of Bleak House) will make 10 pages and a quarter of Household Words. Fifteen pages of my writing, will make a sheet of Bleak House.

A page and a half of my writing, will make a page of Household Words.

The Quantity of the story to be published weekly, being about five pages of Household Words, will require about seven pages and a half of my writing.

and at the head of the first number plan he has, subsequently, written:

Write and calculate the story in the old monthly N⁰ˢ.

These calculations conceal the real difficulty. They amount to saying that one monthly number is the equivalent of four weeklies; but they do not emphasize that the weekly number is now the unit, and that within its brief limits characters must be presented, background sketched, and atmosphere created. A monthly number of thirty-two pages had been a convenient unit for two or three episodes; one or two episodes had now to be related in the equivalent of eight pages. It is no wonder that Dickens found himself hampered. In February he wrote to Forster:

> The difficulty of the space is CRUSHING. Nobody can have an idea of it who has not had an experience of patient fiction-writing with some elbow-room always, and open places in perspective. In this form, with any kind of regard to the current number, there is absolutely no such thing.[3]

The sense of this restriction never left him: "I am in a dreary state," he told Wills on 18 April, "planning and planning the story of *Hard Times* (out of materials for I don't know how long a story)" [4] and in the end he was forced to enlarge his weekly stints to ten pages of his manuscript.[5]

But though the difficulties of the weekly number exasperated him, and though there is reason to suppose that some material was forcibly excluded, there is no doubt that Dickens was able to adapt his manner to the new conditions, and it might be argued that the discipline was good for him. The necessary shortness of the chapters is matched by an economy in detail, noticeable throughout the novel and especially obvious if the opening chapters of *Hard Times* are compared with the opening chapters of *Bleak House*. It is appropriate, no doubt, that the symbolical fog of *Bleak House* should be more leisurely presented than the symbolical fact of *Hard Times*; but it is difficult to believe that in any monthly novel Dickens would have been content with those mere eight but sufficient words which set the scene, "a plain, bare, monotonous vault of a schoolroom." The initial description of Mr. Gradgrind's square appearance is

---

[3] *Letters*, II, 543.

[4] *Ibid.*, 551.

[5] See below, p. 216, n. 2. [The note referred to here reads: "The demands of the story required additional space for this last monthly number. Dickens's note at the head of the number plan reads: 'Weekly Nᵒˢ to be enlarged to 10 of my sides each—about,' i.e., an extension of about two and a half sheets of manuscript for each weekly number."]

conveyed in a traditional manner, but it is considerably shorter than the initial descriptions of Sir Leicester Dedlock and Mr. Tulkinghorn in *Bleak House,* chapter ii; and more remarkable still, both in economy and in power, is the symbolically contrasting appearance of Sissy Jupe and Bitzer as the sunlight plays upon them:

> whereas the girl was so dark-eyed and dark-haired, that she seemed to receive a deeper and more lustrous color from the sun, when it shone upon her, the boy was so light-eyed and light-haired that the self-same rays appeared to draw out of him what little color he ever possessed. His cold eyes would hardly have been eyes, but for the short ends of lashes which, by bringing them into immediate contrast with something paler than themselves, expressed their form. His short-cropped hair might have been a mere continuation of the sandy freckles on his forehead and face. His skin was so unwholesomely deficient in the natural tinge, that he looked as though, if he were cut, he would bleed white.

It is not merely that Bitzer's body has been deprived by Coketown smoke of the life-giving sun, or that his mind has been repressed by a lifeless education, but that he is emptier and shallower than Sissy; there is no depth to him. The monthly novels are not without comparable moments. The juxtaposition of Miss Flite and the young wards at the end of *Bleak House,* chapter iii, is equally well contrived, she suitably enough at the *bottom* of the steep, broad flight of stairs, they looking down upon her, and her words are equally powerful to suggest more than they say,

> Youth. And hope. And beauty. And Chancery. And Conversation Kenge! Ha! Pray accept my blessing!

This, however, is only a small part of a much larger episode. It lacks the rounded completeness of the scene in *Hard Times.*

But though Dickens recognized how his manner required adapting to weekly presentation, he was also determined to "write and calculate the story in the old monthly N^{os}." This is shown not only by the memorandum but by the whole appearance of the manuscript. In it the novel is divided into five monthly parts, each separately foliated as his custom was when writing a monthly serial, and each represented by a separate number plan. The first of these makes clear that after deciding what shall happen during the month he arranged this material in chapters before distributing the chapters into weekly issues. He evidently felt the need to see these chapters grouped into units larger than a weekly number, even though the monthly unit could not force itself upon the reader's attention and might not even be apparent to him. These larger monthly units would serve as stages by which to measure the progress made and the distance still to be covered. Thus the opening words of chapter viii, the last of the first monthly "part"—"Let us strike the key-note again, before pursuing the tune"—seem to indicate that the exposition is completed; and the ending of the second "part" with Louisa Gradgrind's marriage to Bounderby, the third with Stephen Blackpool leaving Coketown, and the fourth with the breakdown of Louisa's marriage, all mark important stages completed in the development of the story.

Though the reader may appreciate the completion of the stage without observing that a monthly "part" is completed also, his attention is called to still larger movements in the story by the division of the novel into "books." The device had frequently been used since its adoption from the epic by Fielding in *Joseph Andrews*. But Dickens had not hitherto employed it.[6] Perhaps he had taken notice of Thackeray's refinement in *Esmond* (1852) of not merely numbering his books, as the custom was, but of naming them. The second number plan of *Hard Times* shows him considering this device ("republish in 3 books? / 1. Sowing / 2. Reaping / 3. Garnering"). By then it was perhaps too late to adopt it in serial publication: we do not know whether the first weekly issue, without an indication of book number, was already in print when the second monthly "part" was under consideration. But the notion was kept in mind, and when the novel was reissued in volume form it was divided into books with the titles already determined, the divisions coinciding with what had been the end of the second and fourth monthly "parts."

Of earlier novels, only *Dombey and Son* lends itself to a similar division, with well-marked stages reached at the end of Number V (the death of Paul), Number X (Mr. Dombey's second marriage), and Number XV (the flight of Florence). But from *Hard Times* onwards each novel, except for *Edwin Drood,* is divided into books even in the serial issues. This is further evidence of the attention which Dickens was now paying to construction. He was quite justified in telling Carlyle that *Hard Times* was "constructed . . .

---

[6] Except in the serial version of *Oliver Twist,* of which ch. xxii in Part XI is numbered the first of the Second Book. The book-division of this novel was abandoned in the first "volume" edition.

patiently, with a view to its publication altogether in a compact cheap form." [7]

II

Dickens's first purpose was to establish the dominion of Fact and of its high priest, Mr. Gradgrind. The draft titles show that Mr. Gradgrind was to be the representative of a theory. It is therefore appropriate that he should first appear in his own school impressing his theories upon the rising generation, who will show the effect of his teaching as the story develops.

Although Dickens had settled upon the name, opinions, and perhaps the nature of his principal character before beginning to write, he was still undetermined about his supporters. Mr. Gradgrind was to have two children—the first number plan specifies "Louisa Gradgrind" and "Young Thomas"—who would doubtless exist to disappoint him in different ways; but whether his wife was still alive was not yet decided. Dickens was evidently tempted to produce another repellent widower with a sister in attendance, as Miss Murdstone had attended upon Mr. Murdstone, and Mrs. Chick upon Mr. Dombey. The number plan shows his purpose settling: "Mrs. Gradgrind—or Miss? Wife or Sister? Wife." Having fixed upon that, he turned to consider the remainder of the household: "Any little Gradgrinds?

Say 3. Adam Smith ⎫
　　　 Malthus　　⎬ no parts to play"
　　　 Jane　　　 ⎭

Jane Gradgrind is later to play a small, yet not unimportant, part; and Mrs. Gradgrind is to become one more of Dickens's ineffectual mothers, closer in type to Mrs. Matthew Pocket in the future than to Mrs. Nickleby in the past. Her entry is carefully timed—postponed from chapter iii ("Mrs. Gradgrind—badly done transparency, with not enough light behind it. No not yet") to chapter iv ("Now, Mrs. Gradgrind"). No member of his household could have had less effect upon Mr. Gradgrind or upon his children, and that was perhaps the reason that she displaced the sister in Dickens's choice: she serves to emphasize more powerfully than any sister that Mr. Gradgrind alone influenced the course of his children's career.

[7] *Letters*, II, 567.

Gradgrind is to be recognized not only in his house and family, but also by the company he keeps. He is seen in school with a representative of the Department of Practical Art, who in his determination to remove flowers from the design of carpets and foreign birds and butterflies from the design of crockery, is as anxious as Gradgrind to submit the imagination to the chains of fact and real circumstance. But the representative of the Department of Practical Art has served a limited purpose by the end of chapter ii, and no more is seen of him.[8]

Much more prominent among Gradgrind's friends is Josiah Bounderby, for whose appearance the reader's expectations are raised at the end of the first weekly number (chapter iii). "What would Mr. Bounderby say?" cried Mr. Gradgrind on finding his elder children peeping through a hole in the circus tent. But Dickens himself had not pronounced the name with equal confidence when meditating his number: "What will Mr. Bound say?" is the version on the number plan (and in the manuscript of chapter iii), subsequently altered to "Bounder" and finally to "Bounderby." Dickens may already have known his man; certainly the very next entry on the number plan shows that he knew what parts he was to play ("Mr. Bounderby, the Bully of humility. Dawn of Bounderby and Louisa"), and in their partnership Gradgrind supplies the ethos of heartless calculation in which Bounderby can oppress the Coketown operatives; but the momentary hesitation over his name shows that Bounderby was not so prominent in Dickens's scheme as Gradgrind.

A final entry on the first number plan points to Gradgrind's third associate: "The man who, being utterly sensual and careless, comes to very much the same thing in the end as the Gradgrind school? Not yet." This was James Harthouse, who is not introduced until the third month. He is a young man of good family who had found army and diplomatic life a bore, and had now been persuaded by an elder brother in Parliament to "go in" for statistics, make a place for himself amongst the "hard Fact fellows," and canvass one of the industrial seats. Finding Coketown as much of a bore as the army and the diplomatic service, he whiles away his time there by attempting to seduce Louisa Bounderby. If Dickens had already foreseen this rôle, it is surprising that he should have contemplated introducing Harthouse in the first month, since he

---

[8] See further K. J. Fielding, "Charles Dickens and the Department of Practical Art," *Modern Language Review*, xlviii (1953), 270–77.

could not perform his function in the plot until Bounderby and Louisa were married. A possible explanation is that Dickens, with his mind on the fable, needed Harthouse as a supporter to Gradgrind; but recognizing that Harthouse could best be employed as a seducer of Louisa, he permitted the requirements of the fable to give place temporarily to the requirements of the plot.

Bounderby also has his supporter. Just as Captain Cuttle is incomplete without Mrs. MacStinger and Captain Bunsby, and Mr. Toots without the Game Chicken, so Bounderby is incomplete without Mrs. Sparsit. The distance he has reached from the humblest origins, born in a ditch and abandoned by his mother, is most readily measured by his now employing as a housekeeper this lady of seemingly the highest family connexions. But Mrs. Sparsit's aristocratic connexions are of doubtful authenticity, and so are Bounderby's origins. The reader is left to guess this and merely to suspect that the eminently respectable countrywoman, Mrs. Pegler, is betraying a suspiciously maternal interest in a most unlovable millowner. Dickens is already preparing the ground for the scene of Bounderby's exposure, or rather of his deflation, for at his first appearance he is seen to have

> a great puffed head and forehead, swelling veins in his temples, and such a strained skin to his face that it seemed to hold his eyes open, and lift his eyebrows up. A man with a pervading appearance on him of being inflated like a balloon, and ready to start.[9]

But though all but the most unsophisticated reader can see that a rich retribution is in store for Bounderby, this assumption of humility on his part and of gentility on Mrs. Sparsit's serves a more immediate purpose. Here at the very centre of the dominion of Fact are people indulging in Fancy, a peculiarly repulsive Fancy maybe, but Fancy still. Here, in the punning of one of the rejected titles, is a man proud of his head but flourishing his tale. This apposition of Fact and Fancy is forcibly presented throughout the first three weekly parts. The young Gradgrinds have been brought up on Fact, but when we first meet them they are contriving to satisfy their starved Fancy by peeping through a hole in a circus tent. Coketown too is "Fact, fact, fact, everywhere in the material aspect of the town; fact, fact, fact, everywhere in the immaterial"; but in an obscure corner of Coketown, Fancy is ensconced in the shape of a circus. The district is so obscure that Mr. Gradgrind and

[9] Ch. IV.

Mr. Bounderby, like two evil characters in *The Pilgrim's Progress,*
do not know where to find it and are forced to enlist the help of
the clown's daughter. The circus people are lodged at an inn named,
in a suitable frolic of Fancy, the Pegasus's Arms, and are expert in
all sorts of fanciful behaviour, in dancing upon rolling casks, stand-
ing upon bottles, catching knives and balls, twirling hand-basins,
and dancing upon the slack wire and the tight-rope. But for all
that they are the salt of the earth:

> there was a remarkable gentleness and childishness about these
> people, a special inaptitude for any kind of sharp practice, and an
> untiring readiness to help and pity one another, deserving often of
> as much respect, and always of as much generous construction, as
> the every-day virtues of any class of people in the world.

And their leader, Mr. Sleary, has a philosophy adapted to the
world of Fancy just as Mr. Gradgrind's is adapted to the world of
Fact:

> "People must be amuthed, Thquire, thomehow," continued Sleary,
> rendered more pursy than ever, by so much talking; "they can't be
> alwayth a working, nor yet they can't be alwayth a learning. Make the
> betht of uth; not the wurtht. I've got my living out of the horthe-
> riding all my life, I know; but I conthider that I lay down the
> philothophy of the thubject when I thay to you, Thquire, make the
> betht of uth: not the wurtht!" [10]

This is the milieu from which Sissy comes to be an inmate of the
Gradgrind household, there to be educated in Mr. Gradgrind's
system. It is some measure of the man's inherent goodness that he
receives her as an inmate. He is redeemable, and the course of the
novel shows that he will be redeemed by Sissy. He fails to educate
her head, but she succeeds in educating his heart.

[10] Ch. VI.

Critique of Materialism

by Edgar H. Johnson

Hard Times brings to a culmination an orderly development of social analysis that extends in Dickens's work from *Dombey and Son* through *Bleak House*. That development has its roots, indeed, far earlier, and is to be found, although fragmentarily, in the social attitudes underlying *Oliver Twist* and the prison scenes of *Pickwick Papers*. With *Dombey and Son*, however, Dickens achieved his first clear picture of the workings of a monetary society; and even while he was still writing that story he underlined his hostility to Mr. Dombey's world through Scrooge and the fantasy of *A Christmas Carol*. Although *David Copperfield* is mainly an exploration of personal emotion, the social comment is an organic part of its pattern. It lurks in the legal morasses of Doctors' Commons and runs through the conscienceless exploitation of child labor in the bottling warehouse; its emphasis on money is as clear in the ostentatious display of Mr. Spenlow as in the mean rapacity of Uriah Heep; its spiritual essence is painted in Steerforth's cynical middle-class indifference to the humanity of the poor and the callousness of his seduction of Little Em'ly.

Bleak House carries on that analysis to a detailed examination of the rotten workings of the social system in almost every major institution and activity of society. Except for one: the operations of that colossus of mechanized industry that had swollen its dominion until it had almost all of modern society subjected to its power. That power Dickens saw as an inhuman, life-denying tyranny. *Bleak House* reveals the monstrous tentacles of acquisitive power in general, crushing human fulfillment in its foggy coils. *Hard Times*

"Critique of Materialism." *From* Charles Dickens: His Tragedy and Triumph *by Edgar H. Johnson (Boston: Little Brown and Company, 1952)*, II, *801–19*. *Copyright 1952 by Edgar H. Johnson. Reprinted by permission of the publisher.* [*The editor has abridged several of the author's longer quotations from* Hard Times. *Otherwise, Professor Johnson's chapter is reprinted in its entirety.*]

deals with industrial power, but is not so much a picture of its ramifications as a presentation of its underlying principles. It is an analysis and a condemnation of the ethos of industrialism.

These facts partly explain why *Hard Times* has been unpopular with many readers and has been disliked by most critics. People could laugh unrestrainedly at Dick Swiveller and Pecksniff and Micawber, who can only amuse, not hurt us, but no such irresponsible mirth is possible with Bounderby and Gradgrind, who have the world appallingly under their control. In Dickens's earlier novels it had been easy to think of him as a warm-hearted, unphilosophic humanitarian indignant at individual cruelties. Even in *Bleak House* the reader might not realize the total meaning of the indictment, and could comfort himself by imagining that Dickens was merely prejudiced against some groups in society—lawyers, money-lenders, members of the aristocracy, politicians. But there is a desperate endeavor among commentators to ignore or belittle the dark masterpieces of Dickens's maturity because they will not let us close our eyes on the clamorous problems that threaten us with disaster. The harsh truth of Mr. Merdle and the Circumlocution Office in *Little Dorrit* is dismissed as "twaddle," and *Our Mutual Friend's* astringent satire on Podsnap and the Veneerings as mere clowning in a dusty desert of a book. Except for a few critics such as F. R. Leavis, who do not care for Dickens's earlier work, only radicals and revolutionaries like Ruskin and Bernard Shaw have praised *Hard Times.*

For in *Hard Times* there is no mistaking Dickens's violent hostility to industrial capitalism and its entire scheme of life. Here he is proclaiming a doctrine not of individual but of social sin, unveiling what he now sees as the real state of modern society. "This," Shaw says, "is Karl Marx, Carlyle, Ruskin, Morris, Carpenter, rising up against civilization itself as a disease, and declaring that it is not our disorder but our order that is horrible; that it is not our criminals but our magnates that are robbing and murdering us; and that it is not merely Tom-all-Alone's that must be demolished and abolished, pulled down, rooted up, and made for ever impossible so that nothing shall remain of it but History's record of its infancy, but our entire social system." "Here you will find," Shaw continues, "no more villains and heroes, but only oppressors and victims, oppressing and suffering in spite of themselves, driven by a huge machinery which grinds to pieces the people it should nourish and ennoble and having for its directors the basest and most foolish of us instead of the noblest and most farsighted." And thus, he summarizes, the indignation with which Dickens began "has spread and deepened into a passionate revolt against the whole industrial order of the modern world." [1]

The change that reaches its climax in *Hard Times*, however, is not only in revolutionary thought, it is in method as well. And this disturbs still another group of Dickens's readers, grown used to a profusion of comic episode and a tremendous crowded canvas thronged with characters almost as numerous as life itself, all painted in vivid contrasting scenes of light and dark with a brilliant external realism. This is the method of *Dombey* and of *Bleak House,* those complicated and elaborate literary structures like some enormous medieval building whose bays and wings and niches are filled with subordinate figures and with bright genre groups of all kinds clustering in a hundred patterns ranging from grotesque fancy to portraits from nature.

Had Dickens been following this method in *Hard Times*, he would have had scenes among the clerks in Bounberby's bank like those in Mr. Dombey's countinghouse and scenes among the hands in Bounderby's factories like those of pasting on the labels in Murdstone and Grinby's warehouse. He would have had scenes of a cotton spinner getting tangled in the threads of his loom as comic as the marchioness smiting herself on the chin with her corkscrew, and extended scenes of clamorous industrial activity as vivid as the brief glimpses of glaring furnace mouths in Little Nell's nocturnal wandering through the Black Country. He would have had scenes of the home lives of the factory laborers as warm as those of the Toodle family, and as grim as those of the brickmakers in *Bleak House.* All this would have been no less easy for Dickens's creative vitality, perhaps even easier, than the technique he did follow. Dictated partly, no doubt, by the need of compressing his story into a short novel of brief weekly installments, that technique was even more determined by Dickens's resolution to make it a formidable and concentrated blow against the iniquity of a heartless materialism.

In consequence, *Hard Times* is a morality drama, stark, formalized, allegorical, dominated by the mood of piercing through to the underlying *meaning* of the industrial scene rather than describing it in minute detail. Therefore Coketown, which might be Hanley,

[1] [George Bernard] Shaw, Introduction to *Hard Times* [London, 1912].

Preston, Birmingham, or Leeds, or, for that matter, Fall River or Pittsburgh, is drawn once for all in a few powerful strokes:

> It was a town of red brick, or of brick that would have been red if the smoke and ashes had allowed it; but as matters stood it was a town of unnatural red and black like the painted face of a savage. It was a town of machinery and tall chimneys, out of which interminable serpents of smoke trailed themselves for ever and ever, and never got uncoiled. It had a black canal in it, and a river that ran purple with ill-smelling dye, and vast piles of buildings full of windows where there was a rattling and a trembling all day long, and where the piston of the steam-engine worked monotonously up and down like the head of an elephant in a state of melancholy madness. It contained several large streets all very like one another, and many small streets still more like one another, inhabited by people equally like one another, who all went in and out at the same hours, with the same sound upon the same pavements, to do the same work, and to whom every day was the same as yesterday and tomorrow, and every year the counterpart of the last and the next. (I, v)

*   *   *

Every packed detail of this entire setting is surcharged with significant emotional and intellectual comment, and every character among the small unified group, symbolic and stylized, who act out their drama in the gritty industrial world, serves to deepen and intensify the meaning. Josiah Bounderby, banker and manufacturer, is its blatant greed and callous inhumanity in action. Thomas Gradgrind retired wholesale hardware dealer, man of facts and figures, is the embodiment of utilitarian economic theory and its endeavor to dry up life into statistical averages. Young Thomas Gradgrind, devoted first and only to his own advantage, is the mean product of the paternal theories—"that not unprecedented triumph of calculation which is usually at work on number one." (I, ix) The daughter Louisa is their predestined tragic victim going to her doom, in her face "a light with nothing to rest upon, a fire with nothing to burn." (I, iii) The consummate achievement of Mr. Gradgrind's system is represented by Bitzer, one of the pupils graduated from the day school founded by Gradgrind: for Bitzer everything is a matter of bargain and sale, accessible to no appeal except that of self-interest.

In contrast to these, Sissy Jupe, the strolling juggler's child, spending her childhood among the acrobats and equestrians of Sleary's Horse-riding, symbolizes everything in human nature that transcends the soul-crushing hideousness and mere instrumentalism of Coketown: she is vitality, generosity, uncalculating goodness. It is significant that she has been born and nourished among a people whose activities are not dominated by pure utility, but have at least some association with those of art, self-fulfilling, self-justified, and containing their ends within themselves. The contrast between her "dark-eyed and dark-haired" (I, ii) warmth, glowing with an inward sun-filled luster, and Bitzer's cold eyes and colorless hair and etiolated pallor, renders in pure sensation, as F. R. Leavis points out, the opposition between "the life that is lived freely and richly from the deep instinctive and emotional springs" and "the thin-blooded, quasi-mechanical product of Gradgrindery." [2]

Nor does Dickens concern himself in *Hard Times* with any of the small tricks of verisimilitude in speech. The characters express themselves in a stylized idiom that is as far removed from everyday diction as it is true to the inward essence of their natures. Louisa speaks in a solemn poetry filled from the beginning with vibrant forewarnings of her destiny, and Sissy, the stroller's child, confronts Harthouse, the smart, sarcastic worldling, with the stern justice of an angelic messenger. Bounderby's housekeeper, Mrs. Sparsit, with her Roman nose and Coriolanian eyebrows, has a grotesque and mournful dignity of utterance fitting to a world of mad melodrama. And in the wild exuberance of his humor, Dickens allows Mr. Bounderby to talk with the extravagant absurdity of a figure in an insane harlequinade. When Mrs. Sparsit, rendered inarticulate by an inflamed throat and pathetic with sneezes, is trying in vain to tell Mr. Gradgrind that Louisa has deserted Bounderby for Harthouse, the aggrieved husband seizes and shakes her. "If you can't get it out, ma'am," he exclaims, "leave *me* to get it out. This is not a time for a lady, however highly connected, to be totally inaudible, and seemingly swallowing marbles." (III, iii)

In all Dickens's previous novels there had been scenes in which the characters burst into a theatrical diction of an ornate dignity or talked a gabble fantastically ridiculous. Nicholas and Ralph Nickleby assail each other in words of purple rhetoric and Edith Dombey addresses both her husband and Mr. Carker in the accents of a tragedy queen, but the successes Dickens achieves in such passages are won in the teeth of their language. And with Mrs. Nickleby, Sampson Brass, Pecksniff, Sairey Gamp, Captain Cuttle,

[F. R.] Leavis [*The Great Tradition* (London, 1948)], p. 231.

Mr. Toots, and Jack Bunsby he had risen to heights of triumphant nonsense. "But now," as Shaw remarks, "it is no longer a question of passages;"—or even of an occasional character—"here he begins at last to exercise quite recklessly his power of presenting a character to you in the most fantastic and outrageous terms, putting into its mouth from one end of the book to the other hardly a word which could conceivably be uttered by any sane human being, and yet leaving you with an unmistakable and exactly truthful portrait of a character that you recognize at once as not only real but typical." [3]

In the same way, the overtones of symbolism and allegory had always moved through Dickens's earlier novels, in solution, as it were, and only at times rendered in definite statement. They are implicit in the social myth of Little Nell's mad grandfather and his mania for the "shining yellow boys" seen against the stock-market-gambling fever of the 1840's. They glimmer in the Christmas pantomime transformation-scenes that end *Martin Chuzzlewit*, with old Martin as the beneficent Prospero bringing the pageant to a close. They are symmetrically balanced in the ice and frozen cupids of Mr. Dombey's dinner table and the warmth of the Little Midship-man where Florence and Captain Cuttle are the wandering princess and the good monster of a fairy tale. They emerge again in the image of Uriah Heep as an ugly and rebellious genie and Betsey Trotwood as the fairy godmother. They underlie that entire sym-bolic bestiary of wolves, tigers, cats, captive birds, flies, and spiders that moves among the fog and falling tenements and self-consum-ing rottenness of *Bleak House*. But in these novels, except for the last, the symbolism always lurked below the surface or played over it in a fanciful and exuberant embroidery of metaphor. Even in *Bleak House* symbolism had never taken charge, nor determined and limited every detail in the structure.

Hard Times opens, significantly, in a schoolroom. Here the chil-dren are to be indoctrinated in the tenets of practicality, encouraged to think of nothing except in terms of use, crammed full of informa-tion like so many "little vessels . . . ready to have imperial gallons of facts poured into them until they were full to the brim." "Now, what I want," Mr. Gradgrind tells the schoolmaster, "is, Facts. Teach these boys and girls nothing but Facts. Facts alone are

[3] Shaw, Introduction.

wanted in life. Plant nothing else and root out everything else. You can only form the minds of reasoning animals upon Facts: nothing else will ever be of service to them. This is the principle on which I bring up my own children, and this is the principle on which I bring up these children. Stick to Facts, sir!" (I, i)

In the Gradgrind world there are to be no imagination, no fancy, no emotion, only fact and the utilitarian calculus. When Sissy Jupe—"Girl number twenty," Mr. Gradgrind calls her, obliterating human identity itself in the blank anonymity of a number —defends her taste for a flowery-patterned carpet by saying, "I am very fond of flowers . . . and I would fancy——" the government inspector of schools pounces upon her triumphantly: "Ay, ay, ay! But you mustn't fancy. That's it! You are never to fancy"; and "You are not, Cecilia Jupe," Mr. Gradgrind repeats sepulchrally, "to do anything of that kind." "Fact, fact, fact!" says the government official. "Fact, fact, fact!" echoes Thomas Gradgrind. (I, ii)

For Sissy's loving humanity, though, this bleak factuality is quite impossible. " 'Here are the stutterings,' " she misquotes her schoolteacher—"Statistics," corrects Louisa—of a town of a million inhabitants of whom only twenty-five starved to death in the course of a year. What does she think of that proportion? "I thought it must be just as hard on those who were starved whether the others were a million, or a million million." So "low down" is Sissy in "the elements of Political Economy" after eight weeks of study, that she has to be "set right by a prattler three feet high, for returning to the question, 'What is the first principle of this science?' the absurd answer, 'To do unto others as I would that they should do unto me.' " (I, ix)

Mr. Gradgrind's stand at school is the stand he takes among his own children at home:

> No little Gradgrind had ever seen a face in the moon; it was up in the moon before it could speak distinctly. No little Gradgrind had ever learnt the silly jingle, Twinkle, twinkle, little star; how I wonder what you are! No little Gradgrind had ever known wonder on the subject, each little Gradgrind having at five years old dissected the Great Bear like a Professor Owen, and driven Charles's Wain like a locomotive engine-driver. No little Gradgrind had ever associated a cow in a field with that famous cow with the crumpled horn . . . or with that yet more famous cow who swallowed Tom Thumb: it had never heard of these celebrities, and had only been introduced

to a cow as a graminivorous ruminating quadruped with several stomachs." (I, iii)

But the facts in which Gradgrindery is interested are only the cut-and-dried facts of intellectual definition, not the facts of living and breathing reality. It wants to learn nothing about the behavior of horses and how they are trained, which Sissy Jupe knows from Sleary's Horse-riding: "You musn't tell us about the ring, here." Instead, it trots out Bitzer's "definition of a horse": "Quadruped. Graminivorous. Forty teeth, namely twenty-four grinders, four eye-teeth, and twelve incisive. . . . Hoofs hard, but requiring to be shod with iron. Age known by marks in mouth."—"Now girl number twenty," says Mr. Gradgrind, "you know what a horse is." (I, ii)

The factual education approved by Mr. Gradgrind is identical in spirit with that which was inflicted upon John Stuart Mill and which left him in his young manhood despairingly convinced that his emotional and imaginative nature had been starved to death.[4] Mr. M'Choakumchild, the schoolmaster, has been "turned out," with "some one hundred and forty other schoolmasters . . . in the same factory, on the same principles, like so many pianoforte legs. . . . Orthography, etymology, syntax, and prosody, biography, as-tronomy, geography, and general cosmography, the sciences of com-pound proportion, algebra, land-surveying and levelling, vocal music, and drawing from models, were all at the ends of his ten chilled fingers. He had worked his stony way into Her Majesty's most Honourable Privy Council's Schedule B, and had taken the bloom off the higher branches of mathematics and physical science, French, German, Latin, and Greek. He knew all about all the Water Sheds of all the world (whatever they are), and all the his-tories of all the peoples, and all the names of all the rivers and mountains, and all the productions, manners, and customs of all the countries, and all their boundaries and bearings on the two and thirty points of the compass. . . . (I, ii)

*   *   *

The principles that dominate Mr. Gradgrind's school are the principles that dominate Coketown and its industry. His hard-facts philosophy is only the aggressive formulation of the inhumane

---

[4] [For a contradictory assessment of Mill's education, see K. J. Fielding's "Mill and Gradgrind" on pp. 111–114 of this volume.]

spirit of Victorian materialism. In Gradgrind, though repellent, it is honest and disinterested. In Bounderby, its embodiment in the business world, with his bragging self-interest, it is nothing but greed for power and material success, Victorian "rugged individualism" in its vulgarest and ugliest form. And Bounderby is nothing but the practice of that business ethos, for which "the relations between master and man were all fact, and everything was fact between the lying-in hospital and the cemetery, and what you couldn't state in figures, or show to be purchaseable in the cheapest market and saleable in the dearest was not, and never should be, world without end, Amen." (I, v)

The wonderful wit and insight with which Dickens withers laissez-faire capitalism is not to be lost sight of "because he chooses to speak," as Ruskin says, "in a circle of stage fire." [5] Carlyle never voiced a more burning denunciation of the dismal science of classical economic theory or the heartlessness of "cash-nexus" as the only link between man and man. The hundred years that have passed since *Hard Times* was written have done hardly more to date the cant with which businessmen defend industrial exploitation than they have to brighten the drab and brutal thing. Laboring men who protested wanted "to be set up in a coach and six and to be fed on turtle soup and venison, with a gold spoon" (I, xi); the laboring class "were a bad lot altogether, gentlemen," "restless," "never knew what they wanted," "lived upon the best, and bought fresh butter; and insisted upon Mocha coffee, and rejected all but prime parts of meat, and yet were eternally dissatisfied and unmanageable." (I, v) As for the Labor unions: "the united masters" should not "allow of any such class combinations." (II, i)

One more cluster of these sardonic clichés recalls the capitalists of our own day who were going to dispose of their businesses and go to Canada if Franklin Delano Roosevelt were re-elected. The Coketown industrialists, Dickens observes dryly, were always crying that they were ruined:

> They were ruined, when they were required to send labouring children to school; they were ruined when inspectors were appointed to look into their works; they were ruined, when such inspectors considered it doubtful whether they were justified in chopping people up with their machinery; they were utterly undone when it was hinted that perhaps they need not always make quite so much smoke.

[5] Ruskin, XI, 7n [*Cornhill Magazine*, II (1860), 159].

. . . Whenever a Coketowner felt he was ill-used—that is to say, whenever he was not left entirely alone, and it was proposed to hold him accountable for the consequences of any of his acts—he was sure to come out with the awful menace that he would "sooner pitch his property into the Atlantic." This had terrified the Home Secretary within an inch of his life, on several occasions.

However, the Coketowners were so patriotic after all, that they never had pitched their property into the Atlantic yet, but, on the contrary, had been kind enough to take mighty good care of it. (II, i)

The only weaknesses in Dickens's handling of the industrial scene are his caricature of the union organizer Slackbridge and his portrayal of that noble but dismal representative of the laboring classes, Stephen Blackpool. Slackbridge, with his windy and whining rhetoric ("Oh my friends and fellow-countrymen, the slaves of an iron-handed and a grinding despotism! Oh my friends and fellow-sufferers, and fellow-workmen, and fellow-men!") is a figment of imagination. "He was not so honest," Dickens says, as the workers he addressed, "he was not so manly, he was not so good-humoured; he substituted cunning for their simplicity, and passion for their safe solid sense. An ill-made, high-shouldered man, with lowering brows, and his features crushed into an habitually sour expression, he contrasted most unfavourably, even in his mongrel dress, with the great body of his hearers in their plain working clothes." (II, iv)

Such a description is a piece of sheer ignorance, not because union leaders cannot be windbags and humbugs as other politicians can, but because labor organizers are not like Slackbridge and do not talk like him, and did not do so in Dickens's day any more than in ours. Dickens knew human nature too well not to know that fundamentally laboring men were like all men, and he knew domestic servants and artisans working for small tradesmen, but of the class manners and behavior of industrial laborers he had made no more than a superficial observation in some half-dozen trips through the Midlands. He had attended only one union meeting in his life, during the Preston strike in January, 1854. "It is much as if a tramp," Shaw comments with witty but not untruthful exaggeration, "were to write a description of millionaires smoking large cigars in church, with their wives in lownecked dresses and diamonds." [6]

There is a possibility, to be sure, that the brief chapter in which Slackbridge appears was designed to reassure a middle-class audi-

[6] Shaw, Introduction.

ence that might otherwise grow restive and worried over the radical sound of the book. Dickens's own personal support of the labor movement, however, is unequivocally clear. He had already stated in *Household Words* his belief that laborers had the same right to organize that their employers had,[7] and shortly after the conclusion of *Hard Times* he was to appeal to working men to force reforms from the Government.[8] *Hard Times* itself burns with indignant sympathly for the injustice under which the workers suffered and is violent in its repudiation of Bounderby's career and Gradgrind's philosophy.

Hardly less typical of the laboring class than Slackbridge is the independent workman Stephen Blackpool, who is ostracized by his fellow workers for not joining the union and blacklisted by Mr. Bounderby for having the courage to defend their cause. Stephen's isolated stand cuts him off from the support of his own class and the patronage of the factory owners. For all this, it is in Stephen's mouth that Dickens puts a dark summation of the life of the industrial workers: "Look round town—so rich as 'tis—and see the numbers o' people as has been broughten into bein heer, for to weave, an to card, an to piece out a livin', aw the same one way, somehows, twixt their cradles and their graves. Look how we live, and wheer we live, an in what numbers, an by what chances, and wi' what sameness; and look how the mill is awlus a goin, and how they never works us no nigher to ony dis'ant object—'ceptin awlus Death." (II, v)

And to Stephen, too, Dickens gives a denunciation of laissez-faire and the hostile division it creates in society:

> Let thousands upon thousands alone, aw leading the like lives and aw faw'en into the like muddle, and they will be as one, and yo will be as anoother, wi' a black unpassable world betwixt yo, just as long or short a time as sitch-like misery can last. . . . Most o' aw, rating 'em as so much Power, and reg'latin 'em as if they was figures in a soom, or machines: wi'out loves and likens, wi'out memories and inclinations, wi'out souls to weary and souls to hope—when aw goes quiet, draggin' on wi' 'em as if they'd nowt o' th' kind, and when aw goes onquiet, reproachin 'em for their want o' sitch human feelins in their dealins wi' you—this will never do't, sir, till God's work is onmade. (II, v)

[7] *Coll. P. [The Collected Papers of Charles Dickens]*, I, 482; "On Strike," *H.W. [Household Words]*, 2/11/54.

[8] *Ibid.*, 510-13, "To Working Men," *H.W.*, 10/7/54.

When Stephen's crushed body is brought up from Old Hell Shaft, into which he had stumbled, his dying words are as if the crushed people themselves were speaking from the pit into which the modern world had fallen:

> I ha' fell into the pit . . . as have cost wi'in the knowledge o' old fok now livin, hundreds and hundreds o' men's lives—fathers, sons, brothers, dear to thousands an thousands, an keeping 'em fro' want and hunger. I ha' fell into a pit that ha' been wi' th' Fire-damp crueller than battle. I ha' read on't in the public petition, as onny one may read, fro' the men that works in the pits, in which they ha' pray'n and pray'n the lawmakers for Christ's sake not to let their work be murder to 'em, but to spare 'em for th' wives and children that they loves as well as gentlefok loves theirs. When it were in work, it killed wi'out need; when 'tis let alone, it killed wi'out need. See how we die an no need, one way an another—in a muddle—every day! (III, vi)

And, in the end, as if from the depths of Old Hell Shaft, Dickens sounds once more a prophetic warning to the "Utilitarian economists, skeletons of schoolmasters, Commissioners of Fact, genteel and used-up infidels, gabblers of many little dog's eared creeds," lest "in the day of [their] triumph, when romance is utterly driven out" of the souls of the poor, "and they and a bare existence stand face to face, Reality will take a wolfish turn, and make an end of you." (II, vi)

Within this larger sweep of *Hard Times* and its social-economic criticism there is a no less significant spiritual core. That core involves a demonstration of the way in which the Gradgrind philosophy denudes and devastates the life of Mr. Gradgrind himself. Not a bad man, "an affectionate father, after his manner," (I, iii) "Mr. Gradgrind, though hard enough, was by no means so rough a man as Mr. Bounderby. His character was not unkind, all things considered; it might have been very kind indeed if only he had made some mistake in the arithmetic that balanced it years ago." (I, v) Instead, he has gone astray in the aridities of a crude mechanistic theory of human nature, and spends his time in the "parliamentary cinder-heap in London" proving "that the Good Samaritan was a Bad Economist." (II, xii)

His kindness in taking Sissy Jupe under his care enables Dickens to bring in a contrasting picture of the circus folk in Sleary's Horse-riding. They symbolize art, and their position in the eyes of Mr.

Gradgrind and Mr. Bounderby implies the position of art in Victorian England, just as Gradgrind and Bounderby themselves symbolize the orthodox respectability of that society. For them, art is reduced to the status of mere entertainment, and the artist is a useless Bohemian of dubious respectability, whose work they frown on as frivolous and wasteful, utterly valueless for the utilitarian calculus. Nevertheless, that work ministers to vital human needs and, debased and degraded though it is in social estimate, represents one of the few clear links Coketown has with the life of disinterested achievement and the enrichment of experience.

*   *   *

The circus people are also vessels of those simple virtues of sympathy and helpfulness to others for which Mr. Gradgrind's philosophy had no use and Mr. Bounderby's hardened heart no room. When Bounderby harshly tells Sissy that her father has deserted her, "They cared so little for plain Fact, these people," Dickens writes, "and were in that advanced state of degeneracy . . . that instead of being impressed by the speaker's strong common sense, they took it in extraordinary dudgeon. The men muttered 'Shame!' and the women 'Brute!' "—a reaction leading Sleary to give the visitors a hasty warning that they were in danger of being pitched out of the window. (I, v)

There is no sentimentality in this portrayal of the circus strollers. Dickens admits that "they were not very tidy in their private dress" and grants that they were sometimes rather disorderly in their private lives. He knows the dirt and squalor of their surroundings. He sees Sleary exactly as he is, with his flabby body, game eye, wheezing voice, and brandy-soaked state of never being quite sober and never quite drunk. But he knows that the qualities they exemplify are just as real as those in Mr. Gradgrind, and that they are quite as likely to be found in jugglers and acrobats as in bankers and businessmen.

So the two worlds confront each other, the world of generous feeling and the world of rationalized greed. It is through his heartless philosophy that Mr. Gradgrind is to be struck down, and through his inconsistent deed of kindness that he and his family are ultimately to be saved. Through his blindness to imagination, his failure to understand the life of the emotions, the mechanical crudity of his philosophy, his son becomes a selfish sneak and thief, and Louisa, his favorite child, suffers a dark emptiness in her heart.

The love that her father always ignores, the devotion to which he denies any reality, she directs with all her starved and thwarted intensity upon her scapegrace brother. For his sake she accepts the proposal her father brings from Bounderby and prostitutes herself in marriage to a man she does not love.

The scene in which she receives that proposal is a triumph of dramatic subtlety. Her dispassionate chill is disconcerting even to the father who has consistently urged treating every situation in terms of fact. With intervals of silence between them punctuated by the hollow ticking of a "deadly statistical clock," she subjects her father to a cold questionnaire: "Father, do you think I love Mr. Bounderby?" "Father, do you ask me to love Mr. Bounderby?" "Father, does Mr. Bounderby ask me to love him?"

The embarrassed man tries to escape into the realms of abstract definition; the reply, he says, depends "on the sense in which we use the expression." Mr. Bounderby does not do either Louisa or himself "the injustice of pretending to anything fanciful, fantastic, or (I am using synonymous terms) sentimental." Let them reduce the question to one of Fact: "Does Mr. Bounderby ask me to marry him? Yes, he does. The sole remaining question then is: Shall I marry him?" (I, xv)

*   *   *

How beautifully this conversation, in reducing each question to one of "Fact," empties it of all meaning! No philosophic analysis could puncture the calculus of fact with more deadly effectiveness. And with what power it conveys the emotional tensions beneath the dialogue, Louisa's yearning for sympathy and understanding and the obtuse, well-meaning father missing it all, even the allusion to those unquenchable fires of human passion, so often hidden, that burst out in the dark night of despair. An uncomfortable sense of something not quite right, however, Mr. Gradgrind does have, and he questions his daughter whether she has any other attachment:

> What do *I* know, father, of tastes and fancies; of aspirations and affections; of all that part of my nature in which such light things might have been nourished? What escape have I had from problems that could be demonstrated and realities that could be grasped?

As Louisa speaks these words, she unconsciously closes her hand, "as if upon a solid object," and slowly opens it, "as though she were releasing dust or ash." Mr. Gradgrind is "quite moved by his success, and by this testimony to it."

When Louisa's disastrous marriage to the braggart Bounderby ends in flight back to her father, all his past blindness recoils upon his head. "How could you give me life," she reproaches him, "and take from me all the inappreciable things that raise it from the state of conscious death? Where are the graces of my soul? Where are the sentiments of my heart? What have you done, O father, what have you done," and she strikes herself with both hands upon her breast, "with the garden that should have bloomed once, in this great wilderness here!"

"I never knew you were unhappy, my child."

*   *   *

And as he clasps her to prevent her falling, and then lays her down upon the floor, he sees "the pride of his heart and the triumph of his system, lying, an insensible heap, at his feet."

The next day he entreats Louisa to believe that he had meant to do right:

> He said it earnestly, and to do him justice he had. In gauging fathomless deeps with his mean little excise-rod, and in staggering over the universe with his rusty stiff-legged compasses, he had meant to do great things. Within the limits of his short tether, he had tumbled about, annihilating the flowers of existence with greater singleness of purpose than many of the blatant personages whose company he kept.

But in the crisis of his life, Mr. Gradgrind, unlike Sir Austin Feverel, is able to choose love and his child, not the pride of his system. And she finds her comfort and he finds his redemption through the uncalculated and inconsistent deviation from the system that had led to his taking into his household the strolling juggler's child. Sissy Jupe's affection has been twining through that utilitarian home the ministrations of a loving heart, and on her gentle strength both the father and the daughter in the end come to repose. Through Sissy, too, and Sleary's non-utilitarian gratitude for Mr. Gradgrind's kindness to her, comes the resolution of the remaining part of the story, the escape of young Tom, that other "triumph" of Mr. Gradgrind's system, from going to jail for robbing Bounderby's bank.

This conclusion to the demonstration is trenchant satire. Sulky to the last, disguised as a comic servant with black face and a grotesquely ludicrous livery, the whelp grumblingly defends himself in his father's own jargon: "So many people are employed in situations of trust; so many people, out of so many, will be dishon-est. I have heard you talk, a hundred times, of its being a law. How can *I* help laws? You have comforted others with such things, father. Comfort yourself!" (III, vii)

Swift upon this confrontation arrives Bitzer, the real success of the system, determined to drag Tom back to Coketown and clinch his own succession to Tom's job in the bank. To the anguished father's pleas, Bitzer's replies, with mordant irony, throw in his face every one of his old arguments. Has he a heart? Mr. Gradgrind asks. "Smiling at the oddity of the question," Bitzer retorts with brisk factuality that the circulation couldn't be carried on without one. "If this is solely a question of self-interest with you," Mr. Gradgrind begins. But Bitzer interrupts. "I am sure you know that the whole social system is a question of self-interest." Nor can he be bribed; his advancement at the bank is worth more than any sum Mr. Gradgrind can offer. Mr. Gradgrind tries to appeal to Bitzer's grat-itude for his schooling. "My schooling was paid for," says Bitzer; "it was a bargain; and when I came away, the bargain ended." (III, viii)

"It was a fundamental principle of the Gradgrind philosophy," Dickens notes,

> that everything was to be paid for. Nobody was ever on any account to give anybody anything, or render anybody any help without purchase. Gratitude was to be abolished, and the virtues springing from it were not to be. Every inch of the existence of mankind, from birth to death, was to be a bargain across the counter. And if we didn't get to Heaven that way, it was not a politico-economical place, and we had no business there.

Bitzer is prevented from giving the alarm and young Tom is smuggled out of the country by a fantastic plot involving the services of the circus's dancing horse and educated dog. Mr. Sleary, no economist to the last, refuses any financial reward, although a collar for the dog and a set of bells for the horse, he agrees, he will be glad to take. "Brandy and water I alwayth take." And privately, to Mr. Gradgrind, over his glass of grog, he makes a final revelation and pronouncement. Sissy's father is dead: his per-forming dog, who would never have deserted him, had returned to the circus months ago, worn out and almost blind, and there died.

It seems to suggest, Mr. Sleary observes musingly, that there is a love in the world, not all self-interest after all, but something very different; and that love has a way of its own of calculating or not calculating, to which it may be hard to give a name.

And, as for the circus artists and Mr. Gradgrind's former disapproval of them, Mr. Sleary says in his preposterous lisp:

> Thquire, thake handth, firtht and latht! Don't be croth with uth poor vagabondth. People mutht be amuthed. They can't be alwayth a learning, nor yet they can't be alwayth a working, they ain't made for it. You *mutht* have uth, Thquire. Do the withe thing and the kind thing too, and make the betht of uth; not the wortht! (III, viii)

Seen in all its implications against the background of the story, these final scenes hold in solution Dickens's entire indictment of nineteenth-century industrial society and the essence of his defense of art. Against the monstrous cruelty of mine and mill and pit and factory and countinghouse, against the bleak utilitarian philosophy with which they were allied, what power could there be except the flowering of the humane imagination and the ennoblement of the heart?

Hard Times—Dickens's Masterpiece?

by A. O. J. Cockshut

Dr. Leavis has performed a valuable service by focusing attention on *Hard Times,* an important and neglected work. Those of us who do not quite agree with him about its quality are nevertheless grateful.

The leading idea of the book is proclaimed in the contrast between its subject, industrial society, and the titles of its three sections—Sowing, Reaping and Garnering. The intention, carried out at times with great subtlety and at times with a rather weary obviousness, was to show inherent life and growth conquering theory and calculation. This approach tends to break down the stock distinctions between town and country, between industry and agriculture, between science and intuition. From the first brilliant description of the factory world, where the elephants' heads represent the movements of machinery, the factory is treated as a living thing. Thus industrial smoke is linked with the horrors of hypocrisy and deception.

> A blur of soot and smoke, now confusedly tending this way, now that way, now aspiring to the vault of Heaven, now murkily creeping along the earth, as the wind rose and fell, or changed its quarter: a dense formless jumble, with sheets of cross light in it, that showed nothing but masses of darkness: Coketown in the distance was suggestive of itself, though not a brick of it could be seen.

And in a notable passage the fire of the furnaces is compared to the fire of human passions. When she is considering Bounderby's proposal, Louisa is asked by her father, "Are you consulting the chimneys of the Coketown works?" and she replies, "There seems to be nothing there but languid and monotonous smoke. Yet when the night comes, Fire bursts out."

Coketown and its people are living mysteries, not facts. The process of inner growth is never absent from the author's mind. It dominates even casual phrases: "to pretend . . . that they went astray wholly without cause, and of their own irrational wills, was to pretend that there could be smoke without fire, death without birth, harvest without seed." This, in part, is the meaning of Stephen Blackpool's fall into the disused mine, which causes his death. The creature of industrial society, the mine, does not cease to influence events when it is uncontrolled and forgotten—a point which Stephen's own words underline: "When it were in work, it killed wi'out need; when 'tis alone, it kills wi'out need."

Now it seems that two of the three main targets at which Dickens directed his criticism, were well chosen. Bounderby and Harthouse, each in his odd, inverted way, illustrate the principle of inner life and growth. Bounderby's story of character and industry triumphant is a sham; and his mock humility about being brought up in the gutter is a form of snobbery and pride. His relations with Mrs. Sparsit perfecly illustrate the real source of his feelings and his lies. The important point is that the low "down-to-earth" materialistic attitude takes its origin in an idealistic illusion. Harthouse, on the other hand, has adopted the dogmas of political economy out of boredom, out of that weary assumption of originality, which is always a mark of dullness of mind. (How well Dickens understood this *avant-garde* type. Gowan in *Little Dorrit* is a different and equally interesting version of it.) Also Harthouse knows in advance that the devotees of political economy will be secretly impressed with his upper-class connections. Therefore he will carry more weight in their councils than he would in circles more accustomed to enjoying aristocratic support. His pose is one of cynicism. "The only difference between us and the professors of virtue or benevolence, or philanthropy—never mind the name—is, that we know it is all meaningless, and say so; while they know it equally and will never say so." But this sincere-insincerity is itself insincere. He has no real interest in the cynical principles of the political economists; his cynicism is only an attractive line. He is the ancestor of a long line of "brutally frank and courageously outspoken" publicists of the twentieth century; and it can be fairly claimed that Dickens may well have been the first person to understand and analyse the type.

Altogether it is a beautifully-planned contrast between Bounderby and Harthouse. But the third term is surely weaker than Dr. Leavis allows. Gradgrind seems to belong to the world of pure moral fable—which in its main outlines *Hard Times* most certainly is not. So we are uneasy whenever Gradgrind has dealings with Bounderby and Harthouse. They are not the same kind of creature at all, and so can only communicate, as it were, through the author's mind. And so there is no reserve of dramatic force to play with at the time of Gradgrind's conversion; the conversion itself, accordingly, is almost trivial.

Of course, the atmosphere of the moral fable, or even of the fairytale is introduced deliberately at times. We cannot doubt that when we read a sentence like this: "Stephen, whose way had been in a contrary direction, turned about, and betook himself as in duty bound to the red brick castle of the giant Bounderby." It is deliberate, but is it always judiciously used? Neither Bounderby nor Blackpool really deserves this aura of fairytale. Each has his own psychological truth; and each has characteristics which could not occur in any pre-industrial society.

There is a similar difficulty about the circus. Dr. Leavis says, most aptly, of the scene where Sleary finally points the book's moral: "Reading it there we have to stand off and reflect at a distance to recognise potentialities that might have been realised elsewhere as Dickensian sentimentality. There is nothing sentimental in the actual fact." The crucial importance of Mr. Sleary and the circus is obvious. The circus is at the beginning and the end. From it comes Sissy Jupe to save the Gradgrind family; and Tom, the disgraced product of a politico-economical education returns to it to make his escape.

But here again we meet the difficulty, are we reading a fable or a novel? In a semi-realistic work of this sort we can hardly be satisfied with the circus as a simple undifferentiated alpha and omega, like Kafka's castle or the lake from which Arthur's sword appeared and to which it returned. We are bound to look for some positive wisdom in Mr. Sleary and I cannot help feeling that Dr. Leavis is too enthusiastic when he speaks of "the solemn moral of the whole fable, put with the rightness of genius in Mr. Sleary's asthmatic mouth." Sleary belongs, of course, to a long tradition of the wise or holy fool. To speak of genius here is surely to place Sleary among the finest representatives of this tradition, to put him in the company of the Fool in *Lear* and Dostoevsky's Myshkin. He will scarcely

stand the comparison; and the passage Dr. Leavis quotes will hardly
support his claim:

> "Thquire, you don't need to be told that dogth ith wonderful ani-
> malth."
> "Their instinct," said Mr. Gradgrind, "is surprising."
> "Whatever you call it—and I'm bletht if I know what to call it"
> —said Sleary, "it ith athtonithing. The way in which a dog'll find
> you—the dithtanthe he'll come."
> "His scent," said Mr. Gradgrind, "being so fine."
> "I'm bletht if I know what to call it," repeated Sleary, shaking his
> head, "but I have had a dogth find me, Thquire. . . ."

It is generally acknowledged by Dr. Leavis and others that the
Trade Union scenes are not satisfactory; though Dickens achieved
one stroke of prophetic insight, when, in Bounderby's interview
with Blackpool, he showed the subconscious sympathy between owners and Trade Unions linked against individualistic workers.

The parallel between Bounderby's and Blackpool's matrimonial
troubles is unconvincing; and one feels that probability, psychology
and everything else had been sacrificed to symmetry. The last chapter
summarises in a few hundred words events which might fill a whole
novel. Here Dickens's sense of the superiority of life to fact, which
is the guiding star of the novel, up to this point, seems ironically
to have deserted him. Gradgrind could almost have written the
chapter himself.

There are then, it seems to me, sound reasons against considering
Hard Times a masterpiece. But it remains a work of great distinction, which performed for the first time the very important imaginative task of integrating the factory world into the world of nature
and of humanity. And I end with a quotation designed to show
this process at work. It is like a new pastoral tradition miraculously
beginning, in which the Industrial Revolution can really share:

> They walked on across the fields and down the shady lanes, some-
> times getting over a fragment of a fence so rotten that it dropped at
> a touch of the foot, sometimes passing near a wreck of bricks and
> beams overgrown with grass, marking the site of deserted works.
> They followed paths and tracks, however slight. Mounds where the
> grass was rank and high, and where brambles, dockweed, and such
> like vegetation, were confusedly heaped together, they always avoided;
> for dismal stories were told in that country of the old pits hidden
> beneath such indications.

The Social Microcosmic Pattern

by Earle Davis

The second novel in Dickens' dark period continues his indictment of Victorian society. Since *Hard Times* is—of all his books—
the clearest in its statement of his economic beliefs, it naturally
holds the attention of all those readers who find this phase of Dickens' fiction to be the most stimulating in our times. Yet for years
this was the novel most easily dismissed by traditional Dickensians,
since it represents few of the narrative qualities they were accustomed to praise. It it tempting for the modern critic to say that
the traditional Dickensian has been wrong and that *Hard Times*
is an underrated novel. Its thesis is challenging, it contributes materially to Dickens' total study of the social microcosm, but it is something less than a great novel for several reasons. Since it has been
enthusiastically praised by George Bernard Shaw, and since a critic
of the stature of F. R. Leavis thinks it is Dickens' greatest book—
"a completely serious work of art" [1]—one needs to look closely at
the reasons for finding it less effective than *Bleak House* or *Little
Dorrit*.

Several factors must be taken into account in judging *Hard
Times*. It was not meticulously planned; it was written somewhat
hurriedly to fill a blank in the schedule of *Household Words*; and
it was constructed in the weekly and constricted installments with
which Dickens had last contended in *The Old Curiosity Shop* and
Barnaby Rudge. Despite the fact that the thesis of *Hard Times* is

From "The Social Microcosmic Pattern." *From* The Flint and the Flame:
The Artistry of Charles Dickens *by Earle Davis (Columbia, Missouri: University
of Missouri Press, 1963; London: Victor Gollancz, Ltd., 1963), pp. 214–23. Copyright © 1963 by the Curators of the University of Missouri Press. Reprinted by
permission of Laurence Pollinger Limited and the University of Missouri Press.
[This discussion of* Hard Times *is excerpted from a study of* Bleak House, Hard
Times, *and* Little Dorrit.]

[1] F. R. Leavis, *The Great Tradition* [(London, 1948)], p. 273.

an integral part of his narrative intentions in this creative period, he found less room for developing his contrasting plot sequences. He also had difficulty in focusing all his narrative technical resources on his subject, so that the novel does not call upon many of his best devices. One needs a relatively large scope for many contrasting plots in action. The sequences which interlocked the large monthly parts of *Bleak House* had no similar opportunity in the smaller pieces which were required by the magazine's weekly issues. The novel sometimes gives the effect of choppy episodes, of undeveloped contrasts, of unfinished business, and this kind of effect is not exactly characteristic of Dickens' last period of creation.

Dickens was hampered by several other considerations in writing this novel. He evidently intended to discuss unions and strikes at more length, but he had contracted to print a novel by Mrs. Gaskell immediately after his own. He had read her manuscript before he began *Hard Times.* She was using the same subject matter, as anyone who wishes to examine *North and South* can see. Mrs. Gaskell read the installments of *Hard Times* with growing uneasiness, and even seems to have been suspicious (apparently with good reason) that Dickens was stealing her thunder as well as appropriating her material.[2] Her protests must have bothered Dickens.

Hard Times retains force because of its purpose. It is influenced materially by Carlyle's economic ideas; it follows naturally Dickens' attack on legal and social maleficence in *Bleak House,* since economic exploitation was another phase of his case against Victorian society. As the novel stands, its thesis is a satire on utilitarian economy. Dickens felt that a dependence upon capitalistic *practicality* without reference to *sympathy* and *brotherly understanding* causes continued difficulties in the relations of capital and labor. His scene was Manchester or Leeds or some such center of England's industrial revolution, and he called the place Coketown.

Dickens planned three separate plot sequences for his novel, each of them presenting opportunities for development and contrast. His main action was to center around Thomas Gradgrind, a retired wholesale hardware merchant who had become a member of Parlia-

---

[2] [Edgar] Johnson [*Charles Dickens: His Triumph and Tragedy* (New York, 1952)], II, 797. Mrs. Gaskell must have thought it odd that Dickens would begin writing a novel so much like hers in theme when he was contracting to print hers afterwards. Note his letter to her, April 21, 1854, Nonesuch, II, 554. One may conjecture that Dickens liked the theme very much and thought it ought to be handled properly by a good novelist, namely Dickens.

ment. Gradgrind is Mr. Utilitarian, "a man of realities; a man of
facts and calculations; a man who proceeds upon the principle that
two and two are four, and nothing over." [3] Mathematically speaking, with no allowances for the tender or susceptible emotions, Mr.
Gradgrind conducts all the business of life *practically,* because this
is the way one gets ahead, makes money, and becomes financially
and socially successful according to Victorian standards. Mr. Gradgrind bows to Carlyle's God of Cash-Payment, and he intends to
conduct his life and bring up his children according to his philosophy.

The plot divisions show how this utilitarian philosophy works
out. There are four children in the family, plus the adopted Sissy
Jupe. Two of the children (named Adam Smith and Malthus) are
mentioned, then dismissed from the tale. But Louisa, Tom, and
Sissy carry the main action. Louisa is given in marriage to the capitalist, Mr. Bounderby, and is tempted to escape from her resulting
unhappiness by an affair or elopement with Mr. Harthouse, a hand-
some dilettante who offers her admiration and some degree of
excitement. The temptation of Louisa is the first complication in
the Gradgrind plot; Dickens handles it as he had occasionally done
in the past, by showing his heroine on the verge of succumbing to
temptation, but successfully resisting it at the last moment. Certainly Louisa's upbringing and her father's philosophy are of no
help to her. This sequence is a typical intrigue borrowed from the
tradition of sentimental drama.

In contrast, young Tom is ruined by his environment. He is
presented as selfish, ill-natured, sensual, and completely mercenary.
He is employed as a clerk in a bank owned by his sister's husband,
Mr. Bounderby, and eventually steals money from the bank in order
to cover his debts contracted in dissipation and idleness. He contrives a scheme to throw the blame on Stephen, a workman in Mr.
Bounderby's factory, and the resulting action which establishes
Stephen's innocence and fixes the blame properly on Tom brings
the novel to its conclusion.

Sissy Jupe is the daughter of a clown, who deserts her and runs
off from the circus which is playing in Coketown. The father had
grown so old and stiff that he had lost his ability to amuse his
audiences. Thinking his daughter well-situated at the Gradgrind

---

[3] *HT,* Bk. I, chap. ii, p. 490. [Page references to *Hard Times* in this essay are
to the Nonesuch edition of Dickens's works.]

school, he disappears, and Mr. Gradgrind decides to provide for her. Sissy, like a character in a morality play, illustrates all the ideas opposite from the utilitarian philosophy taught at school. If any special intrigue was to have been developed around her, it never finds place in the novel. However, she does shame Mr. Harthouse into leaving the neighborhood just as Louisa seems on the verge of joining him, and she helps Tom escape when he is about to be arrested for stealing, sending him to the circus where Mr. Sleary, the owner, conceals him and gets him safely abroad.

The second division of action centers about Mr. Bounderby, who is an even more vicious portrait of the hardhearted capitalist than was Scrooge or Mr. Dombey. Mr. Bounderby is part of the Louisa-Harthouse triangle, but he also has a separate course of action, based upon his relationship to his housekeeper, Mrs. Sparsit. This lady is from a higher caste and presumably brings social distinction to the home of a man who had made his own money. Since she is destitute, she accepts money from Mr. Bounderby. She nurses an unrequited affection for him which shows itself in jealousy of the young wife he brings home. Bounderby also has a mother he is ashamed of, and there is a small intrigue which shows her visiting Coketown on occasion just to look at her son from a distance. Bounderby thus illustrates false pride as well as a lack of filial affection. He is exposed at the end as having fabricated much of the story he tells about his youth and the lack of opportunities afforded him in his climb to fortune and power.

The third division of action concerns the power-loom weaver, Stephen Blackpool. Stephen is tied to an impossible wife who has drunk herself into a state which defies marital happiness. Stephen loves another woman, Rachael, wants a divorce from his wife, but finding it impossible to secure one, he and Rachael live in a state of frustration. Since it is Stephen who is used by Tom Gradgrind in his scheme to shift responsibility for the theft from the bank, Stephen is connected with the Gradgrind sequence. He refuses to join the union of working-men, suffering ostracism because of this, but he insists on defending his fellow workers when Mr. Bounderby asks him about the union. He is accordingly fired and blacklisted. Dickens then shows him leaving Coketown at the time when he is coincidentally suspected of stealing. He tries to return to defend himself, but falls into an abandoned mine shaft on the way back. He is discovered just before he dies.

These three plot sequences illustrate Dickens' general plan for

revolving his action around his thesis. The thesis is broader than
the attack on utilitarian economy, since it also encompasses criticism
of the educational system, the caste system, and divorce laws. Mr.
Gradgrind's school, conducted by M'Choakumchild, stresses hard
facts and resembles in many respects the forcing school of Dr. Blim-
ber in *Dombey and Son*. Mr. M'Choakumchild knows a little about
everything, but has never learned how to communicate anything
but knowledge for its own sake. Sissy reports to Louisa her difficulties in understanding him in a particularly suggestive passage:

> "And he said, Now, this school room is a Nation. And in this
> nation there are fifty millions of money. Isn't this a prosperous nation?
> Girl number twenty, isn't this a prosperous nation, and an't you in
> a thriving state?"
> "What did you say?" asked Louisa.
> "Miss Louisa, I said I didn't know. I thought I couldn't know
> whether it was a prosperous nation or not, and whether I was in a
> thriving state or not, unless I knew who had got the money, and
> whether any of it was mine. But that had nothing to do with it. It
> was not in the figures at all," said Sissy, wiping her eyes.[4]

The caste system finds satiric emphasis through the story of Mrs.
Sparsit, whose ambition and position in the social scheme are at
variance. Mr. Harthouse shows the decay which comes from rank
without character. The criticism of the divorce law is quite modern,
because it is obvious that one cannot get a divorce in England
without luck, influence, or money. Since Stephen's wife is an impossible matrimonial companion, since she has not even enough
personality to give him reason for divorcing her according to the
law which fixes adultery as the only legal excuse, and since Stephen
has not enough money to circumvent the law, happiness is out of
reach. Dickens had some feelings about his own marital unhappiness
which related to the opinions expressed in the novel.

The plot sequences of *Hard Times* are not so complex as those
of *Bleak House,* nor are they so fully developed. There is a reasonable amount of motivation in the details of Louisa's abortive attrac-
tion for Harthouse, and there is careful preparation for Tom's
theft. Mr. Gradgrind is shown as a man with a heart underneath
his philosophy, for he aids Sissy, and he sees the error of his ways
after his children experience unhappiness or ruin because of his

[4] *HT*, Bk. I, chap. ix, p. 541.

utilitarian philosophy. Louisa is studied with care, and the reader is likely to sympathize with her difficulties. There is mystery and suspense in the circumstances of Tom's theft, and there is sensation in Stephen's death in the mine pit.

But the humor is absent; the caricature technique fights a losing battle; the speech devices are less effective than usual. The shadowy ghost of caricature shows itself in the early description of Gradgrind and of M'Choakumchild. Mrs. Sparsit has a Coriolanian nose and dense black eyebrows. Her great-aunt, Lady Scadgers, is an immensely gross woman who loves meat and possesses a leg which has refused to get out of bed for fourteen years. Probably the best characters in what is usually an effective Dickensian technique are the circus people. Mr. Sleary, the proprietor, is a fat man with one fixed and one loose eye, a voice like a broken bellows, a head which is never either completely sober or sufficiently drunk, and a manner of speaking which is affected by his asthma and comes out in a lisp which makes his speeches difficult to read. Mr. E. W. B. Childers is a horseman with the troupe and is described extravagantly as resembling a centaur "compounded of the stable and the playhouse. Where the one began, and the other ended, nobody could have told with any precision." Master Kidderminster is a dwarf who assists Childers, being carried on the palm of Childers' hand, feet upward, while the daring vaulting act goes on.

The best speech device is given to Slackbridge, the union organizer. He talks in an oratorical manner which capitalizes on all the rhetoric and elocution usually accompanying hypocrisy. He addresses the Coketown hands in this manner:

> But, oh, my friends and brothers! Oh, men and Englishmen, the downtrodden operatives of Coketown! What shall we say of the man—that working-man, that I should find it necessary so to libel the glorious name—who, being practically and well acquainted with the grievances and wrongs of you, the injured pith and marrow of this land, and having heard you, with a noble and majestic unanimity that will make Tyrants tremble, resolve for to subscribe to the Funds of the United Aggregate Tribunal, and to abide by the injunctions issued by that body for your benefit, whatever they may be—what, I ask you, will you say of that working-man, since such I must acknowledge him to be, who, at such a time, deserts his post and sells his flag; who, at such a time, is not ashamed to make to you the dastardly and humiliating avowal that he will hold himself

aloof, and will *not* be one of those associated in the gallant stand for freedom and for Right? [5]

The symbolic atmosphere which distinguishes the total effect of *Bleak House* is much less important in *Hard Times*. In its place is the rhetorical, exclamatory manner of Carlyle, explaining Dickens' effects instead of implying them. It is true that a smoky haze hovers over Coketown, and elsewhere the workers are described as rising in protest and falling in defeat like the sea. Stephen falls into a pit, and Dickens explains the significance of the pit in Stephen's dying speech:

> I ha' fell into th' pit, my dear, as have cost wi'in the knowledge o' old fok now livin', hundreds and hundreds o' men's lives—fathers, sons, brothers, dear to thousands an' thousands, an' keepin' 'em fro' want and hunger. I ha' fell into a pit that ha' been wi' th' Fire-damp crueler than battle. I ha' read on 't in the public petition, as onny one may read, fro' the men that works in pits, on which they ha' pray'n the lawmakers for Christ's sake not to let their work be murder to 'em, but to spare 'em for th' wives and children that they loves as well as gentlefok loves theirs. When it were in work, it killed wi'out need; when 'tis let alone, it kills wi'out need. See how we die an' no need, one way an' another—in a muddle—every day. [6]

Edgar Johnson and several other critics have found effective symbolism in *Hard Times*, but it is difficult to rank this symbolism in the same class with the fog, mist, rain, and spontaneous combustion of *Bleak House*, or with the prison atmosphere of the following novel, *Little Dorrit*. Surely *Hard Times* should be judged on its artistic merits, a statement which means that it should not be underestimated because of its narrative insufficiency, not overestimated because its thesis appeals to the reader who is concerned with weaknesses in the capitalistic system. Even George Bernard Shaw descends to a judgment which he would normally ridicule in the writings of anyone else. He says:

> Here he begins at last to exercise quite recklessly his power of presenting a character to you in the most fantastic and outrageous terms, putting into its mouth from one end of the book to the other hardly a word which could conceivably be uttered by any sane

[5] *HT*, Bk. II, chap. iv, pp. 617–18.
[6] *HT*, Bk. III, chap. vi. p. 739.

human being, and yet leaving you with an unmistakable and exactly truthful portrait of a character that you recognize at once as not only real but typical.[7]

The least one can say in response to this kind of praise is that it is special pleading. Furthermore, it does Dickens' case little good.

Dickens' criticism of the economic system is quite plain. He is obviously opposed to the excesses of selfish capitalism; he knows that too many workers are underpaid. If something is not done to organize our economy so that laborers have a fair chance to make a reasonable living, he states, there will be trouble. These opinions he holds in common with Carlyle. He says:

> Utilitarian economists, skeletons of schoolmasters, Commissioners of Facts, genteel and used-up infidels, gabblers of many dog-eared creeds, the poor you will have always with you. Cultivate in them, while there is yet time, the utmost graces of the fancies and affections, to adorn their lives so much in need of ornament; or, in the day of your triumph, when romance is utterly driven out of their souls, and they and a bare existence stand face to face, Reality will take a wolfish turn, and make an end of you.[8]

This comment indicates that Dickens is aware of the threat of revolution or other violence. Yet Stephen, a sympathetic character, does not join the union. The organizer Slackbridge, in *Hard Times,* is given a most offensive mannerism of speech, and the general impression of the union is that it forms because foolish capitalists will make no concessions to reality. Workers join a union in an effort to protect themselves. Dickens says, in describing the Coketown hands, that when they rise "like a sea," they do harm chiefly to themselves. This is their dilemma. The implication is that strikes and violence do not help in the long run.

Most of the critics who argue that Dickens is a conscious or unconscious radical either ignore Slackbridge or belittle his importance in relation to Dickens' economic views. Edgar Johnson apparently is one of this group:

> Such a description is a piece of sheer ignorance, not because union leaders cannot be windbags and humbugs as other politicians can, but because labor organizers are not like Slackbridge and do not

[7] [George Bernard] Shaw, Introduction to *Hard Times* [London, 1912].
[8] *HT,* Bk. II, chap. v, p. 672.

talk like him, and did not do so in Dickens' day any more than in ours.[9]

It would be possible for ministers to argue that no preacher talks like Chadband, or for servants to argue that no one talks like Sam Weller, or for Dickens' mother to insist that no woman talks like Mrs. Nickleby. It all depends on whose ox is being gored. One must either assume that Dickens did not mean what he was saying in heightened form, or else he was bowing to the opinions of his readers. If either is true, his entire picture of Victorian society loses force, and the reader might as well discount whatever part of the picture he disagrees with.

There is some further evidence which bears upon the problem. In *Household Words* Dickens says that laborers have the same right to organize that their employers have.[10] In another issue he asks working-men to force reforms from the Government.[11] On the occasion when he read *A Christmas Carol* to an audience composed entirely of workingmen and their wives, he made an introductory address in which he said that it was necessary and right for workers to take a share in the management of industry. Cooperation would make an end of exploitation.[12] This view would not startle a Fabian Socialist or a member of England's Labour party, but it would hardly satisfy Lenin.

One last quotation from *Hard Times*. Stephen speaks for Dickens:

> Sir, I canna, wi' my little learning an' my common way, tell the genelmen what will be better aw this—though some workingmen o' this town could, above my powers—but I can tell him what I know will never do 't. The strong hand will never do 't. Vict'ry and triumph will never do 't. Agreeing for to mak' one side unnat'rally awlus and forever right, and t'oother side unnat'rally and forever wrong, will never, never do 't. Nor yet lettin' alone will never do 't.[13]

This is usually taken as an attack upon the laissez-faire system of letting business do what it pleases. But Dickens says that neither side can be always and forever right without reference to the other

[9] Johnson, II, 811. [See Johnson's essay, "Critique of Materialism," reprinted in this volume.]
[10] "Strike," *Household Words*, February 6, 1858, 169–72.
[11] "To Working Men," *Household Words*, October 7, 1854.
[12] Jack Lindsay, Charles Dickens: [*A Biographical and Critical Study* (London, 1950)], p. 300.
[13] *HT*, Bk. II, chap. v, p. 627.

side. He is arguing for what he conceives to be justice to both capital and labor; he is arguing for cooperation; he is saying that Victorian society does not award justice to labor; he is saying that something drastic needs to be done, or revolution will erupt and ruin all.

Dickens as Social Novelist

by Sylvère Monod

The story told in *Hard Times* can be very briefly summarized.
Two sets of characters are presented in clear-cut opposition. There
are, on the one hand, the masters, Gradgrind, theoretician, economist, and Member of Parliament, whose eyes are to be opened at
the end of the novel when the failure of his "system" is made
apparent by the misfortunes and mistakes of his children, and
Bounderby, millowner, self-made man, hard, vulgar, and narrow-
minded, who will turn out to have been a moral impostor. And
there are, on the other hand, the workers, among whom the con-
spicuous figures are Stephen Blackpool, a saint and a martyr, and
his friend Rachael.

Hard Times presents two theses. One is clear enough and has to
do with the divorce laws. Through the agency of Blackpool, whose
wife is a drunkard and almost completely brutish, Dickens voices
his indignation at the costliness of divorce, which remains a priv-
ilege of the rich. He may have been thinking already, in 1854, of
the possible collapse of his own home life, and he may have wished
publicly to assert his position in favor of the easier dissolution of
all unhappy marriages. Yet the case of Blackpool and his wife is so
different from that of Charles and Catherine Dickens that the link
is by no means certain.

The second social purpose of *Hard Times* is less easily defined.
It seems to be concerned with a radical criticism of the very structure of society, that is, according to Dickens, of the oppression of
the poor and of the workers by the rich. But the novelist's attitude

is partly obscured by his wish to attack, simultaneously, a particular school of economic thinkers, so that his conclusions in that direction remain indistinct. Besides, other elements interfere with the clarity and pungency with which his social ideas are expressed in *Hard Times.*

The sincerity of Dickens' social feeling is not to be called in doubt. Few men have been so vividly struck as he was by the sufferings of the poor, by the unfairness of fate, and by the frequent cruelty of privileged people. Some of his statements on these points are quite clear. In *Hard Times,* Stephen Blackpool delivers a speech which has little profundity, but is inspired by sincere emotion:

> Deed we are in a muddle, sir. Look around town—so rich as 'tis—and see the numbers o' people as has been broughten into bein heer, fur to weave, an to card, an to piece out a livin', aw the same one way, somehows, twixt their cradles and their graves. Look how we live, an wheer we live, an in what numbers, an by what chances, and wi' what sameness; and look how the mills is awlus a goin, and how they never works us no nigher to any dis'ant object—ceptin awlus, Death. Look how you considers of us, an writes of us, and talks of us, an goes up wi' yor deputations to Secretaries o' State 'bout us, and how you are awlus right, and how we are awlus wrong, and never had'n no reason in us sin ever we were born. Look how this ha growen, sir, bigger an bigger, broader an broader, harder an harder, fro year to year, fro generation unto generation. Who can look on 't, sir, and fairly tell a man 'tis not a muddle? (Bk. II, chap. v).

Even in the curtailed form in which it is given here, the speech sounds lengthy. But it contains the most complete definition ever given by Dickens of what, according to him, lies at the root of social evil in general.

It should be observed also that the Lancashire dialect used by the character has a twofold effect. In the author's view, it stresses the speaker's simplicity and, as an indirect implication, his sincerity and virtuousness, and thus makes his words more genuine and weighty. But in fact, it also creates a certain distance between the man who is speaking and the author, who does not assume the whole responsibility for his protest. What David Copperfield had been saying about Parliament in intensely and brilliantly Dickensian style had belonged to the author as well as to the character. Blackpool, on the other hand, is a deserving worker, but he has an ignorant mind and a muddled brain, so that Dickens does not take him so unreservedly as his mouthpiece. In any case, the most striking char-

acteristic of Blackpool's speech, when he sums up the social purpose
of the novel, is the extreme vagueness of the reproaches he is
voicing. The two notions on which he lays stress, the confused state
of the system (or "muddle") and the monotony of the workers' lives
("aw the same one way . . . sameness. . . .") can only be regarded
nowadays as secondary aspects of the social problem. George Orwell
was justified in writing that the whole message of Dickens in *Hard
Times* "is one that at first sight looks like an enormous platitude:
If men would behave decently the world would be decent." [1]

It is rather remarkable that the most vigorous paragraph of social
criticism ever written by Dickens should have remained unpub-
lished. It is to be found among some passages deleted from the corrected proofs of the *Curiosity Shop*. In a long, significant fragment,
Dickens commented scathingly on the living conditions of urban
laborers in unwholesome surroundings,

> in places where, let men disguise as they please, no human beings
> can be clean or good, or sober or contented—where no child can
> be born but it is infected and tainted from the hour it draws its
> miserable breath and never has its chance of worth or happiness—in
> such noisome streets they, the tens of thousands, live and die, and
> give birth to others, tens of thousands more, who live and die
> again, never growing better, but slowly and surely worse. . . .[2]

We shall never know why Dickens discarded that passage, whether
the deletion was due solely to technical reasons, or whether Forster,
liberal-minded but ever prudent and moderate, was responsible for
it. Yet it is clear that Dickens, at least in the early years of his career,
was capable of giving free vent to his indignation and of expressing
himself vigorously and efficiently against some specific injustice that
had drawn his attention. But there was a considerable gap between
such isolated outbursts and the ability to forge a coherent theory
in order to solve the problems of society. The gap has not been
bridged in *Hard Times,* in spite of Dickens' resolve to strike a heavy
blow.

When it is applied to specific points, Dickens' criticism sometimes

[1] "Ch. Dickens," *Critical Essays,* 10. Orwell later admitted that the message
"is not such a platitude as it seems," p. 22. [See Orwell's comments on pp. 109–
11 of this volume.]

[2] Corrected proofs for *OCS* [*The Old Curiosity Shop*], Forster Collection [Vic-
toria and Albert Museum, London]. The passage had been intended for chap.
xliv.

hits the target, but does so at the expense of his over-all purpose. The workers' fate is not inevitably to be improved by attacks against certain economic theories. Such is, however, Dickens' oblique method when he criticizes, without naming them, the utilitarians. The best parts of *Hard Times* devoted to that theme are well known. The opening words of the book are a parody of their doctrine: "Now, what I want is, Facts. . . . Facts alone are wanted in life. . . ." The portrait of Thomas Gradgrind is no less characteristic: "Thomas Gradgrind, sir. A man of realities. A man of facts and calculations . . ." (Bk. I, chap. ii). A little later, a quasi-religious reverence for facts is discreetly hinted at through the adaptation of a familiar ejaculation: "Not that they knew . . . anything about an Ogre. Fact forbid!" (Bk. I. chap. iii).

Finally, one cannot ignore the conversation between Mr. Gradgrind and his young daughter Louisa, when the decision is made to have her marry fifty-year-old Bounderby. The arguments put forward by Mr. Gradgrind to convince his daughter and his deliberately dismissing from the debate any sentimental consideration, seem representative of a mind dried up by its habitual worship of a systematic theory. The scene, in spite of its tendency to lapse into caricature, is one of the most successful in the book. To prove to his daughter that she need not take into account the disparity in years between Mr. Bounderby and herself, Mr. Gradgrind tells her:

> Now, what are the Facts of this case? . . . In considering this question, it is not unimportant to take into account the statistics of marriage, so far as they have yet been obtained, in England and Wales. I find, on reference to the figures, that a large proportion of these marriages are contracted between parties of very unequal ages. . . . It is remarkable as showing the wide prevalence of this law, that among the natives of the British possessions in India, also in a considerable part of China, and among the Calmucks of Tartary, the best means of computation yet furnished us by travellers, yield similar results. The disparity I have mentioned, therefore, almost ceases to be disparity and (virtually) all but disappears (Bk. I, chap. xv).

Love, on the other hand, he declares to be in this context irrelevant and calls it a "misplaced expression."

Dickens seems to have harbored great distrust and dislike of all makers of statistics. His feeling is conveyed by a few sentences deleted from the corrected proofs:

It may be one of the difficulties of casting up and ticking off human figures by the hundred thousand, that they have their individual varieties of affections and passions, which are of so perverse a nature, that they will not come, under any rule, into the account.[3]

Dickens' manuscript notes cast some additional light on his intentions in the criticism of economic theories. In the summary of Chapter IV, Mr. Bounderby is called "the bully of humility," a phrase that is not used in the text itself. The doctrine expounded by Gradgrind is defined in the summary of Chapter II merely as "Marlborough House doctrine," and the part to be played by James Harthouse—he is to court Louisa after her marriage—is twice stressed in significant terms. The first sheet of "mems" already mentions "the man who, by being utterly sensual and careless, comes to very much the same thing in the end as the Gradgrind school," and the fourth takes up the same comparison in greater detail: "To shew Louisa, how alike in their creeds, her father and Harthouse are?—How the two heartless things come to the same in the end?—Yes—Do it almost imperceptibly." [4] Dickens' teaching at that point is thus sufficiently clear and presented in an original manner. The use of the epithet "heartless" in the last quoted fragment is revealing. The sentimental aspect of social and economic questions is still the most immediate one for Dickens. His sensibility is more awakened than his thought, and he wishes to appeal to the reader's sensibility rather than to his intelligence.

In any case, the appeal is doomed to remain of questionable efficiency for lack of a precise ideal in favor of which it might have been launched. The positive side of Dickens' social criticism is nonexistent and his thinking far from coherent. This deficiency is most glaring in the chapters devoted to "trade-union" agitation in Coketown. Dickens is known to have repaired to Preston in order to witness the effect of a prolonged strike and to be in touch with the workers' association. His letters and the *Household Words* articles on the subject do not show that he was unfavorably impressed in Preston by clumsy or dishonest popular orators. It is probably, therefore, on account of his unfortunate youthful experiences in the House of Commons and his subsequent lifelong contempt for all

[3] Forster Collection, chaps. i–ix. All the cancelled passages of *HT* are reprinted in the Ford–Monod edition of that novel. [See "Selected Bibliography" on pp. 122–23 of this volume.]

[4] MS of *HT*, Forster Collection.

political bodies that he instinctively distrusted the incipient workers' unions and presented the Coketown "agitators" in a very ugly light. Dickens' attitude can hardly be regarded as surprising. Twelve years later, George Eliot, in *Felix Holt* and in her essays, was to give similar impressions and to preach similar doctrines, though she was undoubtedly a more advanced social writer and thinker than Dickens. But the attitude of Stephen Blackpool, an ardent believer in the workers' cause, yet preferring to be ostracized by his companions and dismissed by his employer rather than join an association whose purposes he approves of, is never satisfactorily accounted for. To Dickens himself, it was enough of a reason that he had "passed a promess" to Rachael to "let such things be." The promise is itself obscured by some inadvertent deletions at proof stage. But even if the cancelled passages had been left to subsist, Stephen's attitude would have been incompletely justified. His attitude is one of the mainsprings of the action, so that a considerable part of the book is unconvincing. Dickens' dislike of the workers' unions seriously impairs the defense of the workers he had intended to effect in his book.

The effectiveness and the convincingness of his arguments are further weakened by another circumstance. It has already been observed more than once that the very poor and the very unhappy, when he presents them in his novels, paralyze Dickens and deprive him of his comic power. He is held back by a mixture of sincere pity and self-consciousness. He will not have the reader laugh at them and therefore bestows on them none of those amiable eccentricities and harmless foibles which render his lower middle class people so attractive, so that his noble-hearted, humble figures, possessed of astonishing virtues, are completely devoid of charm and almost devoid of life. The author's purpose was to have them arouse admiration, but the modern reader tends to find them unspeakably tedious. The deficiency is nowhere so apparent as in *Hard Times,* where the two major victims are Stephen Blackpool and Rachael. About them, the novelist had harbored singular illusions. "I have done what I hope is a good thing with Stephen, taking his story as a whole," [5] he wrote to Forster. Perhaps he had done a good thing in the sense of a well meant and virtuous attempt, but not in the sense of a successful artistic creation.

[5] [John Forster,] *Life of Dickens* (Tauchnitz edition), V, 63 (July 14, 1854), footnote omitted from Everyman's Library edition.

In his preparatory notes for the final number, he referred to Stephen's death as "the great effect" and enthusiastically under-scored these words twice. Yet all the scenes in which Stephen and Rachael take part are sad and dull. They invariably speak in the tone of virtuous people who are all too conscious of their virtue. When Bounderby asks Stephen whether the presence of Mrs. Sparsit is not an impediment to the confidences he is preparing to make: " 'Sir, I hope I never had nowt to say, not fitten for a born lady to year, sin' I were born mysen',' was the reply, accompanied by a slight flush" (Bk. I, chap. xi). Such unalloyed holiness deserves the highest admiration, but it cannot make of the man who practices and flaunts it either an entertaining companion or an attractive fictional character. A little later the same Stephen tells his friend that she is an angel, to which she retorts: "I am, as I have told thee, Stephen, thy poor friend. Angels are not like me. Between them, and a poor woman fu' of faults, there is a deep gulf set. My little sister is among them, but she is changed" (Bk. I, chap. xiii). The little dead sister embarrasses the reader who has been guiltily de-ploring that Rachael was not just a little more "fu' of faults." Dickens reveals none of her faults, for he believes her to have none, so that her very modesty is but one more perfection. But the reader is hindered from complaining of Rachael's lugubrious perfection when Dickens uses his favorite form of sentimental blackmailing and forcibly refers to a child's death.

Stephen's own death is a characteristic example of the stellar pathos to which Dickens remains addicted. A star shines over the last hours of Stephen's life: "It ha' shined upon me. . . . It ha' shined into my mind. I ha' lookn at 't an thowt o' thee, Rachael, till the muddle in my mind have cleared awa, above a bit, I hope" (Bk. III, chap. vi). And the same theme is relentlessly harped upon by narrator and character alike to the end of that slow chapter.

Stephen's faulty grammar is another form of sentimental black-mailing, for the reader cannot refuse to be moved by such ignorance or to see in it the incontrovertible evidence of Stephen's purity of mind. The temporary eclipse of Dickens' comic vein is shown in the fact that Stephen's tone is identical with Uriah Heep's, which David had found intolerable to the point of striking Uriah's cheek, an unequivocal sign of his disapproval. Stephen was certainly meant to please and did please readers a century ago, but the type of the saintly worker, which owed so much to piety and so little to realistic observation, has had its day. Rather than the enthusiastic praise of a nineteenth century critic like Walter Crotch[6] or the narrator's admiring commentaries, the modern reader is likely to echo the words spoken by James Harthouse, Louisa's lover: "An infinitely dreary person he appeared to me to be. Lengthy and prosy in the extreme. It was knowing to hold forth, in the humble-virtue school of eloquence, but I assure you that I thought at the time 'My good fellow, you are overdoing this!' " (Bk. II. chap. x). Were not Harthouse a contemptible person, it would be pleasant to fancy that there was a twinkle of amused sympathy in Dickens' eye while he wrote these words. Yet the most adequate comment on the social significance of Stephen's portrait is to be found in a critical essay by a Frenchman who exclaimed: "What an abyss there is between Stephen's resignation and the malignant tirades which the socialist novelists of France present in their fiction!" [7] The abyss is there, undoubtedly, but it is neither more nor less than the abyss which lies between reality and a certain ideal, between men as they often are and men as, according to Dickens, they ought to be.

Finally, hampered by his distrust of all associations and paralyzed by the unreal pathetic tone he thought it right to adopt, Dickens did not succeed in putting forward a clear, coherent, persuasive thesis. His attitude can be defined as a kind of sentimental socialism. He was conscious of the existence of a problem, but it was one that acted on his emotions rather than on his intelligence, and thus the solutions he contemplated were all of the benevolent, patronizing kind. His idea seems to have been the substitution of Cheerybles for all the Bounderbys of the world. He placed his trust in the kindness of enlightened employers to secure for the worker the decent life to which he had a right, though he did not in fact enjoy it, as Dickens well knew. For he had written in *Hard Times*, "I entertain a weak idea that the English people are as hard-worked as any people upon whom the sun shines" (Bk. I, chap. x). It was a good thing to have that "weak idea" more widely spread and perhaps in the end generally accepted, but Dickens did very little to show the way toward a better state of things.

[6] See W. Walter Crotch, *The Soul of Dickens* (London, 1916), chap. i.

[7] André Joubert, *Charles Dickens, sa vie et ses oeuvres* (Paris, 1872), 16.

The Rhetoric of *Hard Times*

by David Lodge

On every page *Hard Times* manifests its identity as a polemical work, a critique of mid-Victorian industrial society dominated by materialism, acquisitiveness, and ruthlessly competitive capitalist economics. To Dickens, at the time of writing *Hard Times,* these things were represented most articulately, persuasively, (and therefore dangerously) by the Utilitarians. It is easy to abstract the argument behind the novel, and to demonstrate its logical and practical weaknesses. The argument has two stages: (1) that the dominant philosophy of Utilitarianism, particularly as it expresses itself in education, results in a damaging impoverishment of the moral and emotional life of the individual; and (2) that this leads in turn to social and economic injustice, since individuals thus conditioned are incapable of dealing with the human problems created by industrialism. On the level of plot (1) is expounded in terms of the Nemesis which punishes Gradgrind through his children and (2) is expounded in terms of Stephen Blackpool's sufferings. That Dickens makes a connection between the two propositions and the two areas of the plot is made clear in the scene where Blackpool confronts Bounderby and Harthouse, and is challenged to offer a solution for the "muddle" he is always complaining about. Stephen expresses himself negatively. He repudiates the employers' exploitation of their power ("the strong hand will never do't"); their reliance on *laissez faire* ("lettin' alone will never do't"); their withdrawal from social contact with the working classes ("not drawin

From "The Rhetoric of Hard Times." *From* Language of Fiction *by David Lodge (New York: Columbia University Press; London: Routledge & Kegan Paul Ltd., 1966), pp. 145–63. Copyright © 1966 by David Lodge. Reprinted by permission of the publishers. [In his opening paragraphs, here omitted, the author describes the critical controversy surrounding* Hard Times.]

nigh to fok, wi' kindness and patience an' cheery ways . . . will never do't"); and, "most o' aw," their mental habit of regarding the workers as soulless units in the economic machine while inconsistently accusing them of ingratitude if they protest:

> Most o' aw, rating 'em as so much Power, and reg'lating 'em as if they was figures in a soom, or machines; wi'out loves and likens, wi'out memories and inclinations, wi'out souls to weary and souls to hope—when aw goes quiet draggin' on wi' 'em as if they'd nowt o' th'kind, and when aw goes onquiet, reproachin' 'em for their want o' sitch humanly feelins in their dealins wi' yo—this will never do't, Sir, till God's work is onmade. (II, v)

It is clear that Dickens is speaking through Stephen here, and what the speech amounts to in positive terms is a plea for generosity, charity, imaginative understanding of the spiritual and emotional needs of humanity.

While these values have an obvious relevance to the field of personal relations (the Gradgrind-Bounderby circle) they are less viable as a basis for reform of the body politic, because there are no sanctions to ensure their application. They are not—apart from Louisa's abortive attempt to help Stephen—shown in action in the novel vertically through the class structure: Stephen's martyr-like death bears witness to this. Yet Dickens could only offer a disembodied and vaguely defined benevolence as a cure for the ills of Coketown because he had rejected all the alternatives. In his hostile portrait of Gradgrind, Dickens repudiated not only the narrowest kind of Utilitarian rationalism, but also, as House and others have pointed out, the processes by which most of the great Victorian reforms were carried out—statistical enquiry, commissions, reports, acted on by Parliamentary legislation.[1] In his hostile portrait of Slackbridge, and his account of Stephen's ostracism because of his refusal to join the Trade Union, Dickens repudiated the workers' claim to secure justice by collective bargaining. Dickens is, then, opposed to any change in the political and economic structure of society, and places his hopes for amelioration in a change of heart, mind, and soul in those who possess power, who will then disseminate the

---

[1] E.g.: "He (Mr. Gradgrind) then returned with promptitude to the national cinder-heap, and resumed his sifting for the odds and ends he wanted, and his throwing of the dust into the eyes of other people who wanted other odds and ends—in fact, resumed his parliamentary duties." (II, xi).

88 David Lodge

fruits of this change over the lower echelons of society. Dickens's ideal State would be one of "benevolent and genial anarchy." [2]

This is an insecure basis from which to launch a critique of society, and its insecurity becomes all the more obvious when we look outside *Hard Times* to Dickens's journalism of the same period, and find him enthusing over the wonders of Victorian manufacture[3] and expressing surprised admiration for the Preston cotton-workers' conduct of their strike in 1854.[4]

And yet, when all this has been said, and the contradictions, limitations, and flaws in Dickens's argument extrapolated, *Hard Times* remains a novel of considerable polemical effectiveness. The measure of this effectiveness, it seems to me, can only be accounted for in terms of Dickens's rhetoric. This approach should recommend itself to the author of *The Victorian Sage*,[5] a study which shows how many key Victorian writers, disarmed of logic by their opponents, resorted to non-logical methods of persuasion in order to communicate their ideas. In the criticism of fiction we have learned, notably from Wayne Booth, to use "rhetoric" as a term for all the techniques by which a novelist seeks to persuade us of the validity of his vision of experience, a vision which cannot usually be formulated in abstract terms. But in a novel like *Hard Times,* which can be called a *roman à thèse,* rhetoric functions very nearly in its traditional rôle as the vehicle of an argument.

There is another reason why rhetoric seems a particularly useful term in discussing Dickens's work. Not only is the "author's voice" always insistent in his novels, but it is characteristically a public-speaking voice, an oratorical or histrionic voice; and it is not difficult to see a connection between this feature of his prose and his fondness for speech-making and public reading of his works.

I shall try to show that *Hard Times* succeeds where its rhetoric succeeds and fails where its rhetoric fails; and that success and failure correspond fairly closely to the negative and positive aspects, respectively, of the argument inherent in the novel.

[2] "From one point of view Buckle's book can be seen as an attempt to erect the doctrine of *laissez-faire* into a philosophy of history, and to defend civilized society as a state of benevolent and genial anarchy." Humphry House, *op. cit.* [*The Dickens World* (Oxford, 1941)], pp. 173–74, commenting on H. T. Buckle's *History of Civilization* (1857–61), quoted with approval by Dickens in 1869.

[3] See House, *op. cit.,* p. 166.

[4] See note 8, below.

[5] [John Holloway. See note 9, below, and "Selected Bibliography" in this volume.]

The very first chapter of *Hard Times* affords an excellent illustration of Dickens's rhetoric, and it is short enough to be quoted and analysed in its entirety.

HARD TIMES

BOOK THE FIRST. SOWING

CHAPTER I

THE ONE THING NEEDFUL

"Now, what I want is, Facts. Teach these boys and girls nothing but Facts. Facts alone are wanted in life. Plant nothing else, and root out everything else. You can only form the minds of reasoning animals upon Facts: nothing else will ever be of any service to them. This is the principle on which I bring up my own children, and this is the principle on which I bring up these children. Stick to Facts, Sir!"

The scene was a plain, bare, monotonous vault of a school-room, and the speaker's square forefinger emphasised his observations by underscoring every sentence with a line on the schoolmaster's sleeve. The emphasis was helped by the speaker's square wall of a forehead, which had his eyebrows for its base, while his eyes found commodious cellarage in two dark caves, overshadowed by the wall. The emphasis was helped by the speaker's mouth, which was wide, thin, and hard set. The emphasis was helped by the speaker's voice, which was inflexible, dry, and dictatorial. The emphasis was helped by the speaker's hair, which bristled on the skirts of his bald head, a plantation of firs to keep the wind from its shining surface, all covered with knobs, like the crust of a plum pie, as if the head had scarcely warehouse-room for the hard facts stored inside. The speaker's obstinate carriage, square coat, square legs, square shoulders—nay, his very neckcloth, trained to take him by the throat with an unaccommodating grasp, like a stubborn fact, as it was—all helped the emphasis.

"In this life, we want nothing but Facts, Sir; nothing but Facts!"

The speaker, and the schoolmaster, and the third grown person present, all backed a little, and swept with their eyes the inclined plane of little vessels then and there arranged in order, ready to have imperial gallons of facts poured into them until they were full to the brim.

This chapter communicates, in a remarkably compact way, both a description and a judgment of a concept of education. This concept is defined in a speech, and then evaluated—not in its own terms, but in terms of the speaker's appearance and the setting. Dickens, of course, always relies heavily on the popular, perhaps primitive, assumption that there is a correspondence between a person's appearance and his character; and as Gradgrind is a governor of the school, its design may legitimately function as a metaphor for his character. Dickens also had a fondness for fancifully appropriate names, but—perhaps in order to stress the representativeness of Gradgrind's views—he does not reveal the name in this first chapter.*

Because of the brevity of the chapter, we are all the more susceptible to the effect of its highly rhetorical patterning, particularly the manipulation of certain repeated words, notably *fact, square,* and *emphasis.* The kind of education depicted here is chiefly characterized by an obsession with facts. The word occurs five times in the opening speech of the first paragraph, and it is twice repeated towards the end of the second, descriptive paragraph to prepare for the reintroduction of Gradgrind speaking—" 'we want nothing but Facts, sir—nothing but Facts' "; and it occurs for the tenth and last time towards the end of the last paragraph. In Gradgrind's speeches the word is capitalized, to signify his almost religious devotion to Facts.

Gradgrind's concept of education is further characterized in ways we can group into three categories, though of course they are closely connected:

(1) It is authoritarian, fanatical and bullying in its application.
(2) It is rigid, abstract and barren in quality.
(3) It is materialistic and commercial in its orientation.

The first category is conveyed by the structure of the second paragraph, which is dominated by "emphasis." This paragraph comprises six sentences. In the first sentence we are told how the "speaker's square forefinger emphasised his observations." The next four, central sentences are each introduced, with cumulative force, by the clause "The emphasis was helped," and this formula, translated

* Mary McCarthy has suggested that an anonymous "he" at the beginning of a novel usually moves the reader to sympathetic identification (Mary McCarthy, "Characters in Fiction," *The Partisan Review Anthology* [1962], pp. 260–61). That the effect is quite the reverse in this example shows that the effect of any narrative strategy is determined finally by the narrator's language.

from the passive to the active voice, makes a fittingly "emphatic" conclusion to the paragraph in the sixth sentence: "all helped the emphasis." This rhetorical pattern has a dual function. In one way it reflects or imitates Gradgrind's own bullying, over-emphatic rhetoric, of which we have an example in the first paragraph; but in another way it helps to *condemn* Gradgrind, since it "emphasises" the narrator's own pejorative catalogue of details of the speaker's person and immediate environment. The narrator's rhetoric is, as it must be, far more skilful and persuasive than Gradgrind's.

The qualities in category (2) are conveyed in a number of geo-metrical or quasi-geometrical terms, *wide, line, thin, base, surface, inclined plane* and, particularly, *square* which recurs five times; and in words suggestive of barren regularity, *plain, bare, monotonous, arranged in order, inflexible*. Such words are particularly forceful when applied to human beings—whether Gradgrind or the chil-dren. The metamorphosis of the human into the non-human is, as we shall find confirmed later, one of Dickens's main devices for conveying his alarm at the way Victorian society was moving.

Category (3), the orientation towards the world of commerce, is perhaps less obvious than the other categories, but it is unmis-takably present in some of the boldest tropes of the chapter: *com-modious cellarage, warehouse room, plantation, vessels, imperial gallons.*

The authoritarian ring of *"imperial"* leads us back from category (3) to category (1), just as *"under-scoring* every sentence with a *line"* leads us from (1) to (2). There is a web of connecting strands between the qualities I have tried to categorize: it is part of the rhetorical strategy of the chapter that all the qualities it evokes are equally applicable to Gradgrind's character, person, ideas, his school and the children (in so far as he has shaped them in his own image).

Metaphors of growth and cultivation are of course commonplace in discussion of education, and we should not overlook the ironic invocation of such metaphors, with a deliberately religious, pro-phetic implication (reinforced by the Biblical echo of the chapter heading, "The One Thing Needful" [6]) in the title of the Book, "SOWING," later to be followed by Book the Second, "REAPING," and Book the Third, "GARNERING." These metaphors are given a further twist in Gradgrind's recommendation to "Plant nothing else and root out everything else" (except facts).

[6] Chapter ii of Book I is called "Murdering the Innocents."

If there is a flaw in this chapter it is the simile of the plum pie, which has pleasant, genial associations alien to the character of Gradgrind, to whose head it is, quite superfluously, applied. Taken as a whole, however, this is a remarkably effective and densely woven beginning of the novel.

The technique of the first chapter of *Hard Times* could not be described as "subtle." But subtle effects are often lost in a first chapter, where the reader is coping with the problem of "learning the author's language." Perhaps with some awareness of this fact, sharpened by his sense of addressing a vast, popular audience, Dickens begins many of his novels by nailing the reader's attention with a display of sheer rhetorical power, relying particularly on elaborate repetition. One thinks, for instance, of the fog at the beginning of *Bleak House* or the sun and shadow in the first chapter of *Little Dorrit.* In these novels the rhetoric works to establish a symbolic atmosphere; in *Hard Times,* to establish a thematic Idea —the despotism of Fact. But this abstraction—Fact—is invested with a remarkable solidity through the figurative dimension of the language.

The gross effect of the chapter is simply stated, but analysis reveals that it is achieved by means of a complex verbal activity that is far from simple. Whether it represents fairly any actual educational theory or practice in mid-nineteenth-century England is really beside the point. It aims to convince us of the *possibility* of children being taught in such a way, and to make us recoil from the imagined possibility. The chapter succeeds or fails as rhetoric; and I think it succeeds.

Dickens begins as he means to continue. Later in the novel we find Gradgrind's house, which, like the school-room, is a function of himself, described in precisely the same terms of fact and rigid measurement, partly geometrical and partly commercial.

> A very regular feature on the face of the country, Stone Lodge was. Not the least disguise toned down or shaded off that uncompromising fact in the landscape. A great square house, with a heavy portico darkening the principal windows, as its master's heavy brows over-shadowed his eyes. A calculated, cast up, balanced and proved house. Six windows on this side of the door, six on that side; a total of twelve in this wing, a total of twelve in the other wing; four and twenty carried over to the back wings. A lawn and garden and an infant avenue, all ruled straight like a botanical account-book. (I, iii)

It has been observed [7] that Dickens individualizes his characters by making them use peculiar locutions and constructions in their speech, a technique which was particularly appropriate to serial publication in which the reader's memory required to be frequently jogged. This technique extends beyond the idiosyncratic speech of characters, to the language in which they are described. A key-word, or group of key-words, is insistently used when the character is first introduced, not only to identify him but also to evaluate him, and is invoked at various strategic points in the subsequent action. Dickens's remarkable metaphorical inventiveness ensures that continuity and rhetorical emphasis are not obtained at the expense of monotony. The application of the key-words of the first chapter to Mr. Gradgrind's house gives the same delight as the development of a metaphysical conceit. The observation that Mrs. Gradgrind, "whenever she showed a symptom of coming to life, was invariably stunned by some weighty piece of fact tumbling on her" (I, iv), affords a kind of verbal equivalent of knock-about comedy, based on a combination of expectancy (we know the word will recur) and surprise (we are not prepared for the particular formulation).

Bounderby offers another illustration of Dickens's use of keywords in characterization. He is first introduced as "a big, loud man, with a stare, and a metallic laugh" (I, iv). The metallic quality is shortly afterwards defined as "that brassy speaking-trumpet of a voice of his" (*ibid.*). His house has a front door with "BOUNDERBY (in letters very like himself) upon a brazen plate, and a round brazen door-handle underneath it, like a brazen full stop" (I, xi). Bounderby's bank "was another red brick house, with black outside shutters, green inside blinds, a black street door up two white steps, a brazen door-plate, and a brazen door-handle full-stop" (II, i). The buildings Bounderby inhabits take their character from him, as Gradgrind's do from him. But here the emphasis is on the brass embellishments which, by the use of the word *brazen* (rather than *brass* used adjectivally) epitomize several facets of his characters: his hardness, vanity, crude enjoyment of wealth, and, most important of all, the fact that he is a brazen liar. (We do not know for certain that he is a liar until the end of the novel; the "brazen" fittings reinforce other hints which prepare us for the revelation.)

The failures of characterization in *Hard Times* are generally fail-

---

[7] Randolph Quirk, "Some Observations on the Language of Dickens," *Review of English Literature*, II (1961), 20–21.

ures in using rhetorical strategies which Dickens elsewhere employs
very successfully. The portrait of Slackbridge, the trade union
demagogue, for instance, seeks to exploit a relationship between
character and appearance in a way which is familiar in Dickens and
well exemplified in the first chapter; but it does so crudely and
clumsily:

> Judging him by Nature's evidence, he was above the mass in very
> little but the stage on which he stood. In many respects he was essen-
> tially below them. He was not so honest, he was not so manly, he was
> not so good-humoured; he substituted cunning for their simplicity,
> and passion for their safe solid sense. An ill-made, high shouldered
> man, with lowering brows, and his features crushed into an habitually
> sour expression, he contrasted most unfavourably, even in his mongrel
> dress, with the great body of his hearers in their plain working
> clothes. (II, iv)

Apart from the vividness of "crushed," the description of Slackbridge is carelessly vague, and we miss the metaphorical inventiveness that characterizes Dickens's best descriptions of people. But the
main error of the passage is the ordering of its material. The rhetorical strategy announced by the opening sentence is that Slackbridge's character is to be read in his appearance. But in fact the
character is read *before* we are given the appearance. It is as if
Dickens has so little confidence in his own imaginative evidence that
he must inform us, over-explicitly, what conclusions we are to draw,
before we come to the evidence. We know from external sources that
Dickens was in a confused state of mind about the trade union movement at the time of writing *Hard Times*,[8] and we can rarely expect

---

[8] House (*op. cit.*, pp. 206–8) says that Dickens deliberately went to Preston to
observe the cotton strike there early in 1854, in order to gather material for
Hard Times, and notes that his report in *Household Words* ("On Strike," 11
Feb. 1854) shows a somewhat surprised respect for the orderly and efficient
conduct of the strikers. K. J. Fielding, in his *Charles Dickens: a critical introduction* (1958) argues (pp. 134–35) that "the conditions described in *Hard Times*
are much closer to the engineering strike of 1852 than to the dispute at Preston"
and quotes a contemporary letter of Dickens:

> As to the Engineers . . . I believe the difficulty in the way of compromise,
> from the very beginning, is not so much with the masters as with the
> men. Honorable, generous and free-spirited themselves, they have fallen
> into an unlucky way of trusting their affairs to contentious men, who work

to receive a balanced account of organized labour from any middle-class Victorian novelist. However, the failure of understanding here reveals itself in the first place as a failure of expression; the portrait of Gradgrind, on the other hand, though it probably derives from an equivalent misunderstanding of Utilitarianism, succeeds.

Another, more significant failure of Dickens's rhetoric is to be observed in the treatment of Tom Gradgrind. In this connection, I must register my disagreement with John Holloway's opinion that "the gradual degeneration of Tom . . . is barely (as in fact it is treated) related to Dickens's major problems in the book, though it is one of its best things." [9] It is gradual (though not very extensively treated) up to the beginning of Book II, by which point we have gathered that Tom, so far from drawing strength of character from his repressive and rationalist upbringing, is turning into a selfish young man prepared to exploit others for his own advantage. He is still a long way, however, from the depravity that allows him to connive at the seduction of his own sister and to implicate an innocent man (Stephen Blackpool) in his own crime. This moral gap is rather clumsily bridged by Dickens in the second chapter of Book II, where he suddenly introduces a key-word for Tom: "whelp."

The Bounderbys are entertaining James Harthouse to dinner. Louisa does not respond to Harthouse's attempts to flirt, but when Tom comes in, late, "She changed . . . and broke into a beaming smile. . . ."

> "Ay, ay?" thought the visitor. "This whelp is the only creature she cares for. So, so!"

---

them up into a state of conglomeration and irritation, and are the greatest pests that their own employers can encounter upon earth.

This is certainly the attitude Dickens adopts in *Hard Times*. But on a more fundamental level he also distrusted the trade unions as a threat to the liberty of the individual. He weakens his own case, however, by making Stephen refuse to join the union because of a mysterious and apparently meaningless promise he has made to Rachel (II, vi.). See Raymond Williams (*op. cit.* [*Culture and Society, 1780–1950*], pp. 99–119) for a discussion of the distrust of organized labour by Victorian novelists who sympathised with the oppressed working classes.

[9] Holloway, *op. cit.* ["*Hard Times,* a History and a Criticism," *Dickens and the Twentieth Century,* ed. John Gross and Gabriel Pearson (London and Toronto, 1962)], p. 171.

The whelp was presented, and took his chair. The appellation was not flattering, but not unmerited. (II, ii)

The chapter ends very shortly afterwards, but Dickens contrives to use the word "whelp" three more times, and the title of the following chapter (II, iii), in which Tom betrays Louisa's situation to Harthouse, is entitled "The Whelp."

"Whelp" is a cliché, and it will be noticed that the word is first used by Harthouse, and then adopted by the novelist in his authorial capacity. When a novelist does this, it is usually with ironical intent, suggesting some inadequacy in the speaker's habits of thought.* Dickens plays on Gradgrind's "facts" to this effect. But in the case of Harthouse's "whelp" he has taken a moral cliché from a character who is morally unreliable, and invested it with his own authority as narrator. This gives away the fact that Tom is being forced into a new rôle halfway through the book. For Tom's degeneration *should* be related to the major problems with which Dickens is concerned in *Hard Times*. According to the overall pattern of the novel, Tom and Louisa are to act as indices of the failure of Mr. Gradgrind's philosophy of education, and should thus never be allowed to stray outside the area of our pity, since they are both victims rather than free agents. But Tom's actions do take him beyond our pity, and diminish the interest of his character.

Perhaps Dickens was misled by feeling the need to inject a strong crime-interest into his story, of which Tom was a handy vehicle; or perhaps he lost his head over the preservation of Louisa's purity (the somewhat hysterical conclusion to Chapter iii, Book II, "The Whelp," seems to suggest this). Whatever the ex-

---

* Compare E. M. Forster, a master of this device, in *A Room with a View* (George Emerson has been indiscreet enough to mention in company that his father is taking a bath):

> "Oh dear!" breathed the little old lady, and shuddered as if all the winds of heaven had entered the apartment. "Gentlemen sometimes do not realise—" Her voice faded away. But Miss Bartlett seemed to understand, and a conversation developed in which gentlemen who did not realise played a principal part. (I, 1)

Much later in the novel, Lucy, engaged to another, is desperately fighting off the advances of George. "What does a girl do when she comes across a cad?" she asks Miss Bartlett.

> "I always said he was a cad, dear. Give me credit for that at all events. From the very first moment—when he said his father was having a bath." . . . She moved feebly to the window, and tried to detect the cad's white flannels among the laurels. (II, 16)

planation, "the whelp," unlike those key-words which organize and concentrate the represented character of individuals and places, acts merely as a slogan designed to generate in the reader such a contempt for Tom that he will not enquire too closely into the pattern of his moral development—a pattern that will not, in fact, bear very close scrutiny.

In the conduct of his central argument, Dickens explicitly calls our attention to a "key-note." The first occasion on which he does so is when introducing the description of Coketown, in Chapter v of Book I, entitled "The Key-note."

> Coketown, to which Messrs. Bounderby and Gradgrind now walked, was a triumph of fact; it had no greater taint of fancy in it than Mrs. Gradgrind herself. Let us strike the keynote, Coketown before pursuing our tune.
> It was a town of red brick, or of brick that would have been red if the smoke and ashes had allowed it; but as matters stood it was a town of unnatural red and black like the painted face of a savage. It was a town of machinery and tall chimneys, out of which interminable serpents of smoke trailed themselves for ever and ever, and never got uncoiled. It had a black canal in it, and a river that ran purple with ill-smelling dye, and vast piles of building full of windows where there was a rattling and a trembling all day long, and where the piston of the steam engine worked monotonously up and down like the head of an elephant in a state of melancholy madness. It contained several large streets all very like one another, and many more small streets still more like one another, inhabited by people equally like one another, who all went in and out at the same hours, with the same sound upon the same pavements, to do the same work, and to whom every day was the same as yesterday and tomorrow, and every year the counterpart of the last and the next.

Dorothy Van Ghent has commented on the effects Dickens gains by investing the inanimate with animation and vice versa. "The animation of inanimate objects suggests both the quaint gaiety of a forbidden life, and an aggressiveness that has got out of control. . . . The animate is treated as if it is a thing. It is as if the life absorbed by things had been drained out of people who have become incapable of their humanity." [10] The description of Coketown illustrates this process. The buildings and machinery of Coketown

---

[10] Dorothy Van Ghent, "The Dickens World: A View from Todgers's," *The Dickens Critics*, ed. George H. Ford and Lauriat Lane, Jr. (Ithaca, N.Y., 1961), p. 214.

are invested with a sinister life of their own, the life of savages, serpents, and elephants (the serpent and elephant images are reiterated at least five times in the novel).[11] The people of Coketown, on the other hand, take their character from the architecture of the town non-metaphorically conceived—"large streets all very like one another, and many small streets still more like one another." They are reduced to indistinguishable units caught up in a mindless, monotonous, mechanical process, superbly represented in the droning repetition of sound and syntax in the last sentence of the passage quoted.

In the rest of this chapter Dickens goes on to say that, despite the efficiency of the town, it was afflicted by *malaise,* social and moral: drunkenness, idleness, irreligion. "Is it possible," he asks, "that there was any analogy between the case of the Coketown populace and the little Gradgrinds?" He goes on to suggest that in both "there was fancy in them demanding to be brought into healthy existence instead of struggling on in convulsions."

The antithesis of "fact and fancy" introduces the chapter (see the quotation above). It has been previously introduced in the schoolroom chapters, where Sissy Jupe's words, "I would fancy——," are rudely interrupted by the government official:

"Ay, ay, ay! But you mustn't fancy," cried the gentleman, quite elated coming so happily to his point. "That's it! You are never to fancy. . . . You are to be in all things regulated and governed . . . by fact. . . . You must discard the word Fancy altogether." (I.ii)

A very similar interruption establishes the same antithesis in slightly different terms in Chapter viii, Book I, "Never Wonder," where Dickens again proposes to strike the key-note:

Let us strike the key-note again, before pursuing the tune.

When she was half a dozen years younger, Louisa had been overheard to begin a conversation with her brother one day, by saying "Tom, I wonder"—upon which Mr. Gradgrind, who was the person overhearing, stepped forth into the light, and said, "Louisa, never wonder!"

Herein lay the spring of the mechanical art and mystery of educating the reason without stooping to the cultivation of the sentiments and affections. Never wonder. By means of addition, subtraction, multiplication and division, settle everything somehow, and never

[11] Chapters I, xi; I, xii; II, i; III, v.

wonder. Bring to me, says M'Choakumchild, yonder baby just able
to walk, and I will engage that it shall never wonder.

The antithesis between fact and fancy (or wonder), is, then, the
dominant key-note of *Hard Times*. It relates the public world of
the novel to the private world, the *malaise* of the Gradgrind-Bounderby circle to the *malaise* of Coketown as a social community; and
it draws together the two stages of the central argument of the
book; the relationship between education in the broad sense and
social health. In this respect Dickens is not so very far removed
from the position of the Romantic critics of industrialist society.
Compare Shelley:

> We have more moral, political and historical wisdom than we
> know how to reduce into practice; we have more scientific and
> economical knowledge than can be accommodated to the just dis-
> tribution of the produce which it multiplies. The poetry, in these
> systems of thought, is concealed by the accumulations of facts and
> calculating processes. . . . We want the creative faculty to imagine
> that which we know. . . . To what but a cultivation of the mechani-
> cal arts in a degree disproportioned to the presence of the creative
> faculty, which is the basis of all knowledge, is to be attributed the
> abuses of all invention for abridging and combining labour, to the
> exasperation of the inequality of mankind? From what other cause
> has it arisen that the discoveries which should have lightened, have
> added a weight to the curse of Adam? Poetry, and the principle of
> Self, of which money is the visible incarnation, are the God and
> Mammon of the world.[12]

There is a real community of feeling between Shelley and Dickens
here: one might almost think that *Hard Times* takes its cue for
the criticism of "the accumulation of facts," "calculating processes"
and "the principle of Self" from the *Defence*. But whereas Shelley
opposes to these things poetry, imagination, the creative faculty,
Dickens can only offer Fancy, wonder, sentiments—though he does
so with the same seriousness and the same intentions as Shelley, as
a panacea for the ills of modern society. It is tempting to relate the
inadequacy of Dickens's concept of Fancy[13] to the discussion famil-

[12] *Peacock's Four Ages of Poetry, Shelley's Defence of Poetry, Browning's
Essay on Shelley*, ed. H. F. B. Brett-Smith (Oxford, 1921), p. 52.
[13] Dickens's commitment to "Fancy" is not restricted to *Hard Times*, as
P. A. W. Collins shows in his very thorough study of Dickens's use of the word:

iar in Romantic criticism of Fancy and Imagination. But it is on the rhetorical level that the inadequacy of Dickens's concept manifests itself. In the first "key-note" chapter, the authorial voice inquiries, with heavy irony, whether we are to be told "at this time of day"

> that one of the foremost elements in the existence of the Coketown working-people had been for scores of years deliberately set at nought? That there was any Fancy in them demanding to be brought into healthy existence instead of struggling on in convulsions? That, exactly in the ratio as they worked long and monotonously, the craving grew within them for some physical relief—some relaxation, encouraging good humour and good spirits, and giving them a vent —some recognized holiday, though it were but for an honest dance to a stirring band of music—some occasional light pie in which even M'Choakumchild had no finger—which craving must and would be satisfied aright, or must and would inevitably go wrong, until the laws of the Creation were repealed? (I, v)

The rhetorical questions here impede and confuse the argument. The parallelism of "which craving must and would be satisfied aright, or must and would inevitably go wrong" is tired and mechanical. A mathematical image is enlisted in arguing *against* the mathematical, calculating faculty: it is precisely Dickens's case in the novel as a whole that the "laws of Creation" are not accountable in terms of "ratios." The vagueness of *"some* relaxation," *"some* recognized holiday" is by no means clarified by the unexciting offer of an "honest dance" or a "light pie" as specific palliatives for the people of Coketown.

Dickens is struggling to assert, here, the existence of a universal need in humanity, a need which arises from quite a different side of man's nature from that which is occupied with the mechanical processes of industrialism, a need which must be satisfied, a need distantly related to that need for poetry which Shelley asserts. But whereas Shelley's "poetry" is a faculty which involves and enhances and transforms the total activity of man—"We must imagine that which we know"—Dickens's Fancy is merely a temporary escape from what is accepted as inevitably unpleasant. It is "relief," "a vent," a "holiday." To be cruel, one might say that Dickens offers the oppressed workers of Coketown bread and circuses: bread in the

---

"Queen Mab's Chariot among the Steam Engines: Dickens and Fancy," *English Studies,* XLII (1961), 78–90.

metaphorical "light pie" and circuses in the "honest dance"—and, of course, in Mr. Sleary's circus.

The realm of Fancy is most vividly evoked by the rhetoric of *Hard Times* in what might be called the "fairy-tale" element of the novel.* Many of the characters and events are derived from the staple ingredients of the fairy-tale, and this derivation is clearly revealed in the language.

Louisa and Tom first figure as the brother and sister who often appear in fairy-tales as waifs, exiles, victims of circumstance, hedged about with dangers (the Babes in the Woods, etc.). As they sit by the fire of their room, "Their shadows were defined upon the wall, but those of the high presses in the room were all blended together on the wall and on the ceiling, as if the brother and sister were overhung by a dark cavern" (I, viii). In their childhood their father wears the aspect of an "Ogre":

> Not that they knew, by name or nature, anything about an Ogre. Fact forbid! I only use the word to express a monster in a lecturing castle, with Heaven knows how many heads manipulated into one, taking childhood captive, and dragging it into gloomy statistical dens by the hair. (I, iii)

Later, Louisa becomes the enchanted princess with a heart of ice, while Tom takes on the rôle of the knave. Harthouse is the demon king, popping up suddenly in the action with mischievous intent, in a cloud of (cigar) smoke:

> James Harthouse continued to lounge in the same place and attitude, smoking his cigar in his own easy way, and looking pleasantly at the whelp, as if he knew himself to be a kind of agreeable demon who had only to hover over him, and he must give up his whole soul if required. (II, iii)

Sissy tells Mrs. Gradgrind that she used to read to her father "About the fairies, sir, and the dwarf, and the hunchback, and the genies" (I, vii); and the circus folk in *Hard Times* are comparable to the chorus of benevolent, comic, grotesque, half-supernatural creatures who inhabit the world of romance and fairy-tale. They

---

* My attention was first directed to this (apart from the characterization of Mrs. Sparsit) by a Birmingham undergraduate, Miss Margaret Thomas. Possibly it has been observed before, but I have not been able to find it in Dickens criticism.

are persistently associated with legend and myth—Pegasus (I, v), Cupid (*ibid.*), Jack the Giant Killer (III, vii), etc. Mr. Bounderby's mother, Mrs. Pegler, "the mysterious old woman" (III, v) is the crone who figures in many fairy tales and who brings about a surprising turn in the action. Mr. Bounderby refers to her as "an old woman who seems to have been flying into the town on a broomstick now and then" (II, viii). But the proper witch of the story, and Dickens's most effective adaptation of a stock-figure from fairy-tale, is Mrs. Sparsit. "Mrs. Sparsit considered herself, in some sort, the Bank Fairy," we are told, but the townspeople "regarded her as the Bank Dragon, keeping watch over the treasures of the mine." Her heavy eyebrows and hooked nose are exploited for vivid effects of cruelty:

> Mr. Bounderby sat looking at her, as, with the points of a stiff, sharp pair of scissors, she picked out holes for some inscrutable purpose, in a piece of cambric. An operation which, taken in connexion with the bushy eyebrows and the Roman nose, suggested with some liveliness the idea of a hawk engaged upon the eyes of a tough little bird. (I, xvi)

She flatters Bounderby to his face, but secretly insults his portrait. She wills Louisa into Harthouse's clutches, figuring Louisa's progress as the descent of a "Giant's Staircase," on which she keeps anxious watch (II, x). The boldest treatment of Mrs. Sparsit as a witch occurs in the scene where she steals through the grounds of Mr. Gradgrind's country house, hoping to catch Louisa and Harthouse together.

> She thought of the wood and stole towards it, heedless of long grass and briers: of worms, snails, and slugs, and all the creeping things that be. With her dark eyes and her hook nose warily in advance of her, Mrs. Sparsit softly crushed her way through the thick undergrowth, so intent upon her object that she would probably have done no less, if the wood had been a wood of adders.
> Hark!
> The smaller birds might have tumbled out of their nests, fascinated by the glittering of Mrs. Sparsit's eyes in the gloom. . . . (II, xi)

When a thunderstorm bursts immediately afterwards, Mrs. Sparsit's appearance becomes still more grotesque:

> It rained now, in a sheet of water. Mrs. Sparsit's white stockings were of many colours, green predominating; prickly things were in

her shoes; caterpillars slung themselves, in hammocks of their own making, from various parts of her dress; rills ran from her bonnet, and her Roman nose. (II, xi)

Traditionally, witches are antipathetic to water. It is appropriate, therefore, that the frustration of Mrs. Sparsit's spite, when she loses track of Louisa, is associated with her ludicrous, rain-soaked appearance (see the conclusion to II, xi).

We may add to these examples of the invocation of fairy tale, the repeated description of the factories illuminated at night as "fairy palaces" (I, x; I, xi; II, i, *et passim*), and Mr. Bounderby's often expressed conviction that his men "expect to be set up in a coach and six, and to be fed on turtle soup and venison and fed with a gold spoon" (I, xi; I, vi; II, i, *et passim*). These phrases contrast ironically with the actual drab environment and existence of the Coketown people.

It is, indeed, as an *ironic* rhetorical device that the fairy-tale element operates most successfully. On one level it is possible to read the novel as an ironic fairy-tale, in which the enchanted princess is released from her spell but does not find a Prince Charming, in which the honest, persecuted servant (Stephen) is vindicated but not rewarded, and in which the traditional romantic belief in blood and breeding, confirmed by a discovery, is replaced by the exposure of Bounderby's inverted snobbery.

In other respects, however, the fairy-tale element sets up unresolved tensions in the novel. It encourages a morally-simplified, non-social, and non-historical view of human life and conduct, whereas Dickens's undertaking in *Hard Times* makes quite opposite demands. Mr. Sleary's ruse for releasing Tom from the custody of Bitzer, for instance (III, viii), is acceptable on the level of fairy-tale motivation: he returns Mr. Gradgrind's earlier good deed (the adoption of Sissy) and scores off an unsympathetic character (Bitzer). But the act is essentially lawless, and conflicts with Dickens's appeals elsewhere in the novel for justice and social responsibility. As long as the circus-folk represent a kind of life that is anarchic, seedy, socially disreputable, but cheerful and humane, they are acceptable and enjoyable. But when they are offered as agents or spokesmen of social and moral amelioration, we reject them. The art they practice is Fancy in its tawdriest form, solemnly defended by Mr. Sleary in terms we recognize as the justification of today's mass entertainers:

> People mutht be amuthed. They can't be alwayth a learning, nor
> yet they can't be alwayth a working, they an't made for it. You
> *mutht* have uth, Thquire. (III, viii)

Sissy is meant to represent a channel through which the values of
the circus folk are conveyed to the social order. But her one positive
act, the dismissal of Harthouse (III, ii), depends for its credibility
on a simple faith in the superiority of a good fairy over a demon
king.

In other words, where Dickens invokes the world of fairy-tale
ironically, to dramatize the drabness, greed, spite and injustice
which characterize a society dominated by materialism, it is a
highly effective rhetorical device; but where he relies on the sim-
plifications of the fairy-tale to suggest means of redemption, we remain unconvinced.

If Dickens's notion of Fancy was attached mainly to fairy-tale and
nursery rhyme (cf. the allusions to the cow with the crumpled horn
and Peter Piper in I, iii), his own art is very much one of Fancy in
the Coleridgean sense: "Fancy has no other counters to play with,
but fixities and definites. The Fancy is indeed no other than a mode
of Memory emancipated from the order of time and space. . . ." [14]
This seems an appropriate description of Dickens's method in, for
instance, the first chapter of *Hard Times,* or in the description of
Coketown, or in the treatment of Mrs. Sparsit as a witch. To appreciate this, is to feel that Coleridge was wrong to depreciate
Fancy as a literary mode; but it is also to understand why Dickens's
greatest achievement as a novelist was his depiction of a disordered
universe in which the organic and the mechanical have exchanged
places, rather than in his attempts to trace moral and emotional
processes within the individual psyche.

In *Hard Times,* Dickens expounds a diagnosis of the ills of
modern industrial society for which no institutions can supply a
cure: society, represented by a group of characters, must therefore
change itself, learning from a group outside the social order—the
circus. But Dickens's characters are incapable of change: the language in which they are embodied fixes them in their "given" con-
dition. They can only die (like Stephen Blackpool) or be broken
(like Mr. Bounderby). Mr. Gradgrind may lose his "squareness,"
but he is left a shadow: he cannot become a Michelin Man, all
circles and spheres. Louisa when her heart has been melted is a

---

[14] Coleridge, *Biographia Literaria,* chap. XIII.

far less convincing character than Louisa with a heart of ice. (This can be quickly seen by comparing the scene of her interview with Gradgrind to discuss Bounderby's proposal (I, xv), rightly singled out for praise by Leavis, with the parallel scene at the end of the book where she returns to her father to reproach him for her up-bringing, and where she is given the most embarrassing lines in the novel to speak (II, xii).) Dickens falters in his handling of the character of Tom Gradgrind precisely because he uses a device for fixing character (*whelp*) to express a process of change.

If *Hard Times* is a polemical novel that is only partially persua-sive, it is because Dickens's rhetoric is only partially adequate to the tasks he set himself.

PART TWO

View Points

George Gissing

A more noticeable omission from his books (if we except the one
novel which I cannot but think a failure) is that of the workman at
war with capital. This great struggle, going on before him all his
life, found no place in the scheme of his fiction. He shows us poor
men who suffer under tyranny, and who exclaim against the hard-
ship of things; but never such a representative wage-earner as was
then to be seen battling for bread and right. One reason is plain:
Dickens did not know the north of England. With adequate knowledge of a manufacturing town, he would never have written so
unconvincingly as in his book *Hard Times*—the opportunity for
dealing with this subject. Stephen Blackpool represents nothing at
all; he is a mere model of meekness, and his great misfortune is
such as might befall any man anywhere, the curse of a drunken
wife. The book is a crude attack on materialism, a theme which
might, of course, have entered very well into a study of the com-
batant working-class. But, as I have already pointed out, the working-class is not Dickens's field, even in London. For the purposes
of fiction, it is a class still waiting its portrayer; much has been
written about it in novels, but we have no work of the first order
dealing primarily with that form of life. Mrs. Gaskell essayed the
theme very faithfully, and with some success; but it was not her
best work. I can recall no working-class figures in English novels
so truly representative as those in Charlotte Brontë's second book.
Given a little wider experience, the author of *Shirley* might have
exhibited this class in a masterpiece such as we vainly look for.

From "The Radical." *From* Charles Dickens: A Critical Study *by George
Gissing (Port Washington, N.Y.: Kennikat Press, Inc., 1966), pp. 242–43. Reprinted by permission of the publisher. [This study originally appeared in
1898; it was republished in 1902, a year before Gissing's death.]*

G. K. Chesterton

His next important book, "Hard Times," strikes an almost unexpected note of severity. The characters are indeed exaggerated, but they are bitterly and deliberately exaggerated; they are not exaggerated with the old unconscious high spirits of Nicholas Nickleby or Martin Chuzzlewit. Dickens exaggerates Bounderby because he really hates him. He exaggerated Pecksniff because he really loved him. "Hard Times" is not one of the greatest books of Dickens; but it is perhaps in a sense one of his greatest monuments. It stamps and records the reality of Dickens's emotion on a great many things that were then considered unphilosophical grumblings, but which since have swelled into the immense phenomenon of the socialist philosophy. To call Dickens a Socialist is a wild exaggeration; but the truth and peculiarity of his position might be expressed thus: that even when everybody thought that Liberalism meant individualism he was emphatically a Liberal and emphatically not an individualist. Or the truth might be better still stated in this manner: that he saw that there was a secret thing, called humanity, to which both extreme socialism and extreme individualism were profoundly and inexpressibly indifferent, and that this permanent and presiding humanity was the thing he happened to understand; he knew that individualism is nothing and non-individualism is nothing but the keeping of the commandment of man. He felt, as a novelist should, that the question is too much discussed as to whether a man is in favour of this or that scientific philosophy; that there is another question, whether the scientific philosophy is in favour of the man. That is why such books as "Hard Times" will remain always a part of the power and tradition of Dickens. He saw that economic systems are not things like the stars, but things like the lamp-posts, manifestations of the human mind, and things to be judged by the human heart.

From "Later Life and Works." *From* Charles Dickens: A Critical Study *by G. K. Chesterton (New York: Dodd, Mead & Co., 1906), pp. 230–32. Copyright © 1906 by Dodd, Mead & Co.; renewal copyright 1906 by Gilbert K. Chesterton. Reprinted by permission of Dodd, Mead & Co. and A. P. Watt & Son.*

George Bernard Shaw

I am a Dickensian if by a Dickensian you mean a person who read all Dickens eagerly in his nonage. I read a good deal of him in my childhood before I dreamt of asking whom a book was by. I was a good deal influenced by him. However, I must own that I do not find that cultivated young people in search of interesting novels, can stand Dickens nowadays.

. . . I regard the books of Dickens's second period, from *Hard Times* to *Our Mutual Friend,* as of much greater importance than those of his first period. They can be read by thoughtful and cultivated adults as serious social history.

The earlier books are, no doubt, still delightful to simple folk, children, and Americans—who are still mostly villagers, even when they live in cities, but are at least literate, unlike our own villagers, who regard reading (perhaps wisely) as an eccentric, an unhealthy habit. The younger Dickens, for all his enormously entertaining character sketches and his incorruptible humanity and contempt for idolatry, is not guiltless of derisive ignorance and the sensationalism of the police intelligence.

The desperate necessity he was under of providing for a large family, and the barbarous lack of artistic culture which was common to him and to his pretentiously educated rivals, made themselves felt until his social conscience deepened into a point at which any sort of shallowness or insincerity became impossible to him.

In my preface to *Hard Times,* written for a recent edition of Dickens's works, I have emphasised the turning point which this story marks in his development from the satirist and reformer into the conscious and resolute prophet, and in the indulgence of his humour which, always riotous and extravagant, became utterly reckless when he realised that humanity is so grotesque that it cannot be caricatured.

From "On Dickens" *by George Bernard Shaw. From* The Dickensian, X, *no. 6 (June, 1914), 150–51. Reprinted by permission of the Society of Authors.*

George Orwell

The central action of Dickens's stories almost invariably takes place in middle-class surroundings. If one examines his novels in detail, one finds that his real subject-matter is the London commercial bourgeoisie and their hangers-on—lawyers, clerks, tradesmen, inn-keepers, small craftsmen and servants. He has no portrait of an agricultural worker, and only one (Stephen Blackpool in *Hard Times*) of an industrial worker. The Plornishes in *Little Dorrit* are probably his best picture of a working-class family—the Peggottys, for instance, hardly belong to the working class—but on the whole he is not successful with this type of character. If you ask any ordinary reader which of Dickens's proletarian characters he can remember, the three he is almost certain to mention are Bill Sykes, Sam Weller and Mrs. Gamp. A burglar, a valet and a drunken midwife—not exactly a representative cross-section of the English working class.

Secondly, in the ordinarily accepted sense of the word, Dickens is not a "revolutionary" writer. But his position here needs some defining.

Whatever else Dickens may have been, he was not a hole-and-corner soul-saver, the kind of well-meaning idiot who thinks that the world will be perfect if you amend a few bye-laws and abolish a few anomalies. It is worth comparing him with Charles Reade,[1] for instance. Reade was a much better-informed man than Dickens, and in some ways more public-spirited. He really hated the abuses he could understand, he showed them up in a series of novels which for all their absurdity are extremely readable, and he probably helped to alter public opinion on a few minor but important points. But it was quite beyond him to grasp that, given the existing form of society, certain evils *cannot* be remedied. Fasten upon this or that minor abuse, expose it, drag it into the open, bring it before

From "Charles Dickens." *From* Inside the Whale and Other Essays *by George Orwell (London: Martin Secker & Warburg, Ltd., 1940), pp. 12–14, and Dickens, Dali and Others by George Orwell (New York: Harcourt, Brace & World, Inc.). Copyright © 1946 by George Orwell. Reprinted by permission of Miss Sonia Brownell, Secker & Warburg, and Harcourt, Brace & World, Inc.*

[1] [Charles Reade (1814–1884), now best-known as the author of *The Cloister and the Hearth* (1861).]

a British jury, and all will be well—that is how he sees it. Dickens at any rate never imagined that you can cure pimples by cutting them off. In every page of his work one can see a consciousness that society is wrong somewhere at the root. It is when one asks "Which root?" that one begins to grasp his position.

The truth is that Dickens's criticism of society is almost exclusively moral. Hence the utter lack of any constructive suggestion anywhere in his work. He attacks the law, Parliamentary Government, the educational system and so forth, without ever clearly suggesting what he would put in their places. Of course it is not necessarily the business of a novelist, or a satirist, to make constructive suggestions, but the point is that Dickens's attitude is at bottom not even *de*structive. There is no clear sign that he wants the existing order to be overthrown, or that he believes it would make very much difference if it *were* overthrown. For in reality his target is not so much society as "human nature." It would be difficult to point anywhere in his books to a passage suggesting that the economic system is wrong *as a system*. Nowhere, for instance, does he make any attack on private enterprise or private property. Even in a book like *Our Mutual Friend,* which turns on the power of corpses to interfere with living people by means of idiotic wills, it does not occur to him to suggest that individuals ought not to have this irresponsible power. Of course one can draw this inference for oneself, and one can draw it again from the remarks about Bounderby's will at the end of *Hard Times,* and indeed from the whole of Dickens's work one can infer the evil of laissez-faire capitalism; but Dickens makes no such inference himself. It is said that Macaulay refused to review *Hard Times* because he disapproved of its "sullen Socialism." Obviously Macaulay is here using the word "Socialism" in the same sense in which, twenty years ago, a vegetarian meal or a Cubist picture used to be referred to as "Bolshevism." There is not a line in the book that can properly be called Socialistic, indeed its tendency if anything is pro-capitalist, because its whole moral is that capitalists ought to be kind, not that workers ought to be rebellious. Bounderby is a bullying windbag and Gradgrind has been morally blinded, but if they were better men the system would work well enough—that, all through, is the implication. And so far as social criticism goes, one can never extract much more from Dickens than this, unless one deliberately reads meanings into him. His whole "message" is one that at first

glance looks like an enormous platitude: If men would behave
decently the world would be decent.

K. J. Fielding

No recent study of Dickens is more thoughtful than Dr. F. R.
Leavis' analytic note on *Hard Times* in *The Great Tradition*. Here
and there one may disagree in detail, but it has justly marked out
the way in which the novel should be read if it is to be understood.
Yet some of his remarks should certainly be questioned before
they pass current as valid. Perhaps the foremost of these is the
statement that, "Thomas Gradgrind . . . had brought up his children on the lines of the experiment recorded by John Stuart Mill as
being carried out on himself" (p. 228). This has already been re-
stated more forcibly by Professor Edgar Johnson, who declares in
his recent biography that, "The factual education approved by Mr.
Gradgrind is identical in spirit with that which was inflicted on
John Stuart Mill" (p. 809). This is surely both unfair to James
Mill and unjustified by what his son wrote in the *Autobiography*.
As far as Dickens had any special target for his satire of Gradgrind's
"factual education," it can hardly have been the system privately
adopted by James Mill, but one that was publicly put into practice
in many of the schools.

There is certainly evidence that such factual cramming went on
in schools, and even that it was encouraged by some of the inspectors. But this is too wide a question to pursue here. One of the
cardinal points in Mill's training, on the other hand, was that he
was *not* "crammed with mere fact." He insists that "mine . . . was
not an education of cram. My father never permitted anything I
learnt to degenerate into a mere exercise of memory" (Worlds
Classics edn., p. 26).

It is true that it might be said to be partly similar "in spirit" to
Mr. Gradgrind's system insofar as it made no appeal whatsoever to
the imagination. Yet Mill goes to some pains in the *Autobiography*

"Mill and Gradgrind" *by K. J. Fielding. From* Nineteenth Century Fiction, XI
*(September, 1956), 148–51. Copyright © 1956 by the Regents of the University
of California. Reprinted by permission of the author and the Regents of the
University of California.*

to explain that the reputation that his father and his followers had for despising poetry was not entirely justified. By the age of twelve Mill had read much of Virgil, almost all of Horace, a good deal of Ovid, the *Iliad* and the *Odyssey* right through, and much else in Greek and Latin. He was made to write verse in English; he went on to compose youthful tragedies; and he read most of the major English poets. Much of this was taught for the wrong reasons, but whatever the spirit in which such a training was given, it was far from being "identical" with the one inflicted on the young Bitzer and the little Gradgrinds.

   This is not to say that Dr. Leavis is wrong in linking Mill's *Autobiography* with *Hard Times*. Its account of his spiritual crisis certainly shows better than anything else how the purpose of the novel was the fundamental criticism of an industrial civilization. It simply remains unlikely that Dickens's educational satire was aimed at James Mill. It is all the more surprising that Dr. Leavis did not bring this out himself, since he has done the important service of drawing attention to Mill's critical essays by reprinting them in his *Mill on Bentham and Coleridge* (1950). For it is there that Mill, himself, attacked the very same educational perversions on which Dickens turned in *Hard Times*. In a brief review, entitled "A Prophecy," he associated his attack with a lament at the hard insistence on the "huckstering virtues," and the absence of the "culture of sympathy" which might be learned from a true education in fiction or romance. Although written sixteen years before *Hard Times,* the "prophecy," or his foreboding at what might come when a new generation had grown up that knew none of the romantic virtues, is so well considered and so close to what Dickens must have had in mind in showing what happened to Thomas Gradgrind and young Bitzer, that it deserves reprinting fully as much as the remarkable essays on Bentham and Mill:

> The time was [Mill wrote in 1838], when it was thought that the best and most appropriate office of fictitious narrative was to awaken high aspirations, by the representation in interesting circumstances, of characters conformable indeed to human nature, but whose actions and sentiments were of a more generous and loftier order than are ordinarily to be met with by everybody in every-day life. But now-a-days nature and probability are thought to be violated, if there be shown to the reader, in the personages with whom he is called upon to sympathize, characters on a larger scale than himself or the persons he is accustomed to meet with at dinner or a quadrille party.

Yet, from such representations, familiar from early youth, have not only the noblest minds in modern Europe derived much of what made them noble, but even the commoner spirits what made them understand and respond to nobleness. And *this* is education. It would be well if the more narrow-minded portion both of the religious and scientific education mongers would consider whether the books which they are banishing from the hands of youth were not instruments of national education to the full as powerful as the catalogues of physical facts, and theological dogmas which they substituted—as if science and religion were to be taught not by imbuing the mind with their spirit, but by cramming the memory with summaries of their conclusions. Not what a boy or girl can repeat by rote, but what they have learnt to love and admire, is what forms their character. The chivalrous spirit has almost disappeared from books of education, the popular novels of the day teach nothing but (what is already too soon learnt from actual life) lessons of worldliness, with at the most the huckstering virtues which conduce to getting on in the world; and for the first time perhaps in history, the youth of both sexes of the educated classes are universally growing up unromantic. What will come in mature age from such a youth the world has not yet had time to see. But the world may rely upon it that catechisms, whether Pinnocks' or the Church of England's, will be found a poor substitute for those old romances, whether of chivalry or of Faery, which if they did not give a true picture of actual life, did not give a false one, since they did not profess to give any, but (which was much better) filled the youthful imagination with pictures of heroic men, and of what are at least as much wanted, heroic women (*Westminster Review*, VI and XXVIII [1838], 468–469).

John Stuart Mill and Dickens might well have agreed in condemning the system of education pursued by James Mill, but this remains uncertain. What is clear is that they both strongly disapproved of "catalogues of physical facts" and learning by heart, and that they associated the system of teaching used in schools with the lessons of worldliness taught by an acquisitive society. Mill actually mentions Pinnocks' textbooks, and the same type of work was undoubtedly in Dickens's mind in writing about the "definition of a horse" in the second chapter of *Hard Times*. It is remarkable, too, that in the *Autobiography* Mill recalls that "in the natural course" of his "mental progress" he obtained "poetic culture of the most valuable kind by means of reverential admiration for the lives and characters of heroic persons" (p. 95). This was evidently not denied him.

The whole point of what both Mill and Dickens had to say was that such a hardening of the spirit was not unique. Similar experience could be found recorded in other Victorian biographies. Certainly Charles Darwin wrote almost as if he was thinking of the chief character of the novel. He lamented that after the age of thirty he lost all enjoyment in poetry: Shakespeare "nauseated" him. He wrote,

> My mind seems to have become a kind of machine for *grinding* general laws out of a large collection of facts, but why this should have caused the atrophy of that part of the brain alone, on which the higher tastes depend, I cannot conceive. . . . The loss of these tastes is a loss of happiness, and may possibly be injurious to the intellect, and more probably to the moral character, by enfeebling the emotional part of our nature (*Autobiography of Charles Darwin,* Thinkers Library [1929], p. 74).

It is evident, in brief, that *Hard Times* is just what Dr. Leavis has said it was, beyond his critical asides: not a satire on the old-fashioned utilitarianism of James Mill, but on a more widespread and even harder philosophy which fostered "the inhumanities of Victorian civilisation."

J. Hillis Miller

In *Hard Times* Dickens dramatizes in strikingly symbolic terms the opposition between a soul-destroying relation to a utilitarian, industrial civilization (in which everything is weighed, measured, has its price, and in which emotion is banished), and the reciprocal interchange of love. If the perpetually clanking machinery of the Coketown mills, which turns men into "hands," is the symbol of one, the "horse-riding," as in Picasso's *Saltimbanques,* is the dominant symbol of the other:

> The father of one of the families was in the habit of balancing the father of another of the families on the top of a great pole; the father of a third family often made a pyramid of both those fathers, with Master Kidderminster for the apex, and himself for the base . . . . They all assumed to be mighty rakish and knowing, they were not very

---

From "Hard Times; Little Dorrit; A Tale of Two Cities." *From* Charles Dickens: The World of His Novels *by J. Hillis Miller (Cambridge, Mass.: Harvard University Press, 1958), pp. 226–27. Copyright © 1958 by the President and Fellows of Harvard College. Reprinted by permission of the publisher.*

tidy in their private dresses, they were not at all orderly in their domestic arrangements, and the combined literature of the whole company would have produced but a poor letter on any subject. Yet there was a remarkable gentleness and childishness about these people, a special inaptitude for any kind of sharp practice, and an untiring readiness to help and pity one another . . . (I, 6).

But the circus here is still only a symbol of a good *society*, that is, of communion around a third thing, the "act." In this relation contact with others is still in a way impersonal, and the individual is still defined by his role, by his cooperative submission to a common activity and goal. In the circus act, as in even the best society, the otherness of other people tends to be submerged.

Lionel Stevenson

In contrast with the diffuse opulence of *The Newcomes*,[1] Dickens's novel of the same year was his briefest and most concentrated. This was partly due to its being published in short weekly installments in *Household Words*, but another reason was that *Hard Times* is more strictly centered upon a single social theme than his other novels, and that he had not absorbed this theme through his pores from childhood onward. He began with the conscious purpose of examining the relationship between industrialists and workers in the new manufacturing cities, and of discrediting the utilitarian philosophy which was the ideological basis of current capitalism. This had been foreshadowed in *Dombey and Son* and *Bleak House*. But in those novels he had started with characters and evolved the social implications; in *Hard Times* the characters are obviously invented to demonstrate the theory. It contains none of the richly elaborated comic figures that live so heartily in his other books. With unwonted caution, Dickens began by studying the reports of the newly organized national system of education, and by visiting a strike-bound midland town to observe industrial conflict at first hand. The characters in the novel are neatly arranged in symmetrical groups, either to represent labor *vs.* capital or to contrast the re-

---

From The English Novel: A Panorama *by Lionel Stevenson (Boston: Houghton Mifflin Company, 1960), pp. 311–12. Reprinted by permission of the publisher.*

[1] [By William Makepeace Thackeray, published serially from 1853 to 1855.]

pressed children of a practical school with the fun-loving denizens of a circus.

The angry scorn for utilitarian economics was derived straight from Carlyle, to whom the novel was dedicated. Mr. Gradgrind, with his gospel of facts and statistics, is a perfect embodiment of Carlyle's chief bogy, the ruthless "logic-grinder." And Dickens is caught in the same dilemma that afflicts much of Carlyle's thinking: being as strong a believer in individual responsibility and freedom of choice as were the proponents of *laissez-faire,* he had no faith in any organized system for promoting human welfare. In the past he had assailed charitable institutions and the Poor Laws; now he turned his guns on the new phenomenon of the labor unions, which he saw as an unwarrantable denial of the worker's right to choose his job. Perhaps the least convincing character in the story is the demagogic union organizer. But almost equally lacking in verisimilitude is the nominal hero, Stephen Blackpool, the honest workman who is sacrificed between the conflicting interests of the union and the employers.

Being the only novel of Dickens that is openly revolutionary in its implications, *Hard Times* was admired by such radical social thinkers as Ruskin and Bernard Shaw; and for its tightly organized structure it has been praised by some modern critics who exalt form as the main criterion of fiction. But most readers have always ranked it lower than Dickens's other works, not for its subversive economic views or even for its depressing picture of human greed, but simply because its characters fail to come alive.

Chronology of Important Dates

	Dickens	Cultural and Historical Events
1812	Charles Dickens born February 7.	Byron, *Childe Harold's Pilgrimage*, Cantos I, II.
1814		Scott, *Waverly*.
1821	Begins irregular education.	Death of Keats: Shelley, *Adonais*.
1824	Labors briefly in a warehouse; father imprisoned three months for debt.	
1824–26	Attends Wellington House Academy.	
1827	Works as office boy for an attorney, learns shorthand.	
1832	Works as newspaper reporter.	Reform Act; deaths of Scott and Goethe.
1833	Publishes, in the *Monthly Magazine*, first of a series of sketches of London life.	Carlyle, *Sartor Resartus*; Lamb, *Last Essays of Elia*.
1836	*Sketches by Boz* published February 7. Marries Catherine Hogarth in April.	Morse's invention of the telegraph.
1836–37	*The Pickwick Papers* published in monthly parts (April, 1836–Nov., 1837); edits *Bentley's Miscellany*, in which *Oliver Twist* appears (Feb., 1837–March, 1839).	Reign of Victoria (1837–1901).
1838	*Nicholas Nickleby* (April, 1838–Oct., 1839).	Inauguration of steamship travel between England and U.S.; first rail train enters London.

1840–41	Edits *Master Humphrey's Clock,* weekly periodical, in which *The Old Curiosity Shop* (1840–41) and *Barnaby Rudge* (1841) appear.	
1842	Lectures in U.S.; publishes *American Notes.*	Browning, *Dramatic Lyrics.*
1843	*Martin Chuzzlewit* (Jan., 1843–July, 1844); *A Christmas Carol.*	Wordsworth named Poet Laureate; Carlyle, *Past and Present;* Ruskin, *Modern Painters,* I; Balzac, *Honoria.*
1846–48	*Dombey and Son* (Oct., 1846–April, 1848).	
1847		C. Brontë, *Jane Eyre;* E. Brontë, *Wuthering Heights;* Thackeray, *Vanity Fair* (1847–48); J. S. Mill, *Political Economy.*
1849–50	*David Copperfield* (May, 1849–Nov., 1850); establishes *Household Words,* weekly periodical.	Tennyson, *In Memoriam* (1850).
1852–53	*Bleak House* (March, 1852–Sept., 1853).	
1854	*Hard Times* published in *Household Words* (April 1–Aug. 12).	Crimean War; Preston strike ends.
1855–57	*Little Dorrit* (Dec., 1855–June, 1857).	
1857		Divorce Act; Trollope, *Barchester Towers;* Baudelaire, *Les Fleurs du Mal;* Flaubert, *Madame Bovary.*
1858	Announces separation from his wife.	
1859	Concludes *Household Words;* edits new weekly, *All the Year Round,* in which *A Tale of Two Cities* appears (April 20–Nov. 26).	Darwin, *Origin of Species;* Eliot, *Adam Bede;* Meredith, *Ordeal of Richard Feverel.*
1860–61	*Great Expectations* (Dec. 1, 1860–Aug. 3, 1861).	

1864–65   *Our Mutual Friend* (May, 1864–Nov., 1865).

1866   Dostoyevski, *Crime and Punishment*; Arnold, *Thyrsis*; Atlantic cable completed.

1867–68   Tours America.   Second Reform Act; Marx, *Das Kapital.*

1870   Dies June 9; buried in Westminster Abbey.

Notes on the Editor and Contributors

PAUL EDWARD GRAY, Assistant Professor of English at Princeton University, has written articles and reviews on fiction and is completing a book on the English novel.

JOHN BUTT was Regis Professor of Rhetoric and English Literature at Edinburgh University. At the time of his death, in November, 1965, he was an editor of The Clarendon Dickens for the Oxford University Press.

G. K. CHESTERTON (1874–1936), a critic of English life and literature, was one of this century's most influential Dickensians. In addition to the study represented in this volume, he wrote *Appreciations and Criticisms of Charles Dickens.*

A. O. J. COCKSHUT, a Fellow in English Language and Literature of Hertford College, Oxford, is the author of *The Unbelievers: English Agnostic Thought, 1840–1890.*

PHILIP COLLINS, Professor of English Literature at the University of Leicester, has written a number of studies of Dickens's works, including *Dickens and Crime.* He serves on the Advisory Board of *Victorian Studies.*

EARLE DAVIS, Professor of English and Head of the English Department at Kansas State University, has edited *Great Expectations* and written numerous articles and pamphlets on Dickens.

K. J. FIELDING, Saintsbury Professor of Modern English Literature at Edinburgh University, has written extensively on Dickens and on *Hard Times.* His full-length studies include *Charles Dickens: A Critical Introduction.*

GEORGE GISSING (1857–1903), the prominent late-Victorian novelist, wrote the Prefaces for *The Rochester Edition of the Works of Charles Dickens.*

HUMPHRY HOUSE, who died in 1955, was Senior Lecturer in English at Wadham College, Oxford. Author of *The Dickens World* and *Coleridge: The Clark Lectures,* he also edited *The Notebooks and Papers of Gerard Manley Hopkins.*

EDGAR JOHNSON, Professor of English Literature at the City University of New York, is now at work on a biography of Sir Walter Scott.

DAVID LODGE, who teaches at the University of Birmingham, England, is the author of three novels: *The Picturegoers*; *Ginger, You're Barmy*; and *The British Museum is Falling Down*.

J. HILLIS MILLER, Professor of English at The Johns Hopkins University, has written numerous critical studies, including *The Disappearance of God* and *Poets of Reality*.

SYLVÈRE MONOD, Professor of English in the Sorbonne, is the author of *Dickens, Romancier* and a recent editor, with George H. Ford, of *Hard Times*.

GEORGE ORWELL (1903–1950) is best known as the author of *Animal Farm* and *1984*.

GEORGE BERNARD SHAW (1856–1950), the great British dramatist, was, typically, among the few who praised *Hard Times* in the first decades of this century.

LIONEL STEVENSON, Professor of English at Duke University, recently edited *Victorian Fiction: A Guide to Research* and contributed a chapter on Thackeray to that volume.

KATHLEEN TILLOTSON, Professor of English at Bedford College, University of London, edited *Oliver Twist* for the new Oxford University Press edition of Dickens's works.

Selected Bibliography

Carnall, Geoffrey, "Dickens, Mrs. Gaskell, and the Preston Strike," *Victorian Studies*, VIII (1964), 31–48. A specialized but informative study of the influence of contemporary events on the composition of *Hard Times*.

Dickens, Charles, *Hard Times,* ed. George Ford and Sylvère Monod. New York: W. W. Norton & Company, Inc., 1966. A newly edited text of the novel and a valuable collection of background material.

Fielding, K. J., "*Hard Times* and Common Things," in *Imagined Worlds: Essays on some English Novels and Novelists in Honour of John Butt,* ed. Maynard Mack and Ian Gregor. London: Methuen & Co. Ltd., 1968, pp. 183–203. An interesting assessment, based on new evidence, of Dickens's views on education.

Gerber, Helmut E., "*Hard Times:* An Experience in Teaching," *College English*, XV (March, 1954), 351–53. A brief, low-keyed analysis, useful for students as well as teachers.

Gilmour, Robin, "The Gradgrind School: Political Economy in the Classroom," *Victorian Studies*, XI (1967), 207–24. A well-researched attack on John Holloway's criticism of *Hard Times* (see below).

Hill, T. W., "Notes on *Hard Times*," *The Dickensian*, XLVIII (1951–52), 134–41, 177–85. A spotty but helpful list of annotations to the novel.

Hirsch, David, "*Hard Times* and F. R. Leavis," *Criticism*, VI (Winter, 1964), 1–16. An effective argument against F. R. Leavis's commendation of *Hard Times*.

Holloway, John, "*Hard Times,* A History and a Criticism," in *Dickens and the Twentieth Century,* ed. John Gross and Gabriel Pearson. London: Routledge & Kegan Paul, Ltd.; Toronto: University of Toronto Press, 1962, pp. 159–74. A provocative historical and critical evaluation.

Leavis, F. R., " '*Hard Times*': An Analytic Note," in *The Great Tradition.* New York: New York University Press (paperback), 1963, pp. 227–48. See "Editor's Note" in the "Introduction" to this volume; also see Leavis's remarks on pp. 19–20 of this edition.

Price, Martin, ed., *Dickens: A Collection of Critical Essays.* Englewood Cliffs, N.J.: Prentice-Hall, Inc., 1967. An excellent companion for the student interested in extending his knowledge of Dickens's works.

Watt, William W., "Introduction," *Hard Times.* New York: Holt, Rinehart & Winston, Inc., 1958. A knowledgeable, well-written introduction to the novel.